2023 Global Financial Turbulence and Economic Outlook

Jiandong Ju
Editor

2023 Global Financial Turbulence and Economic Outlook

Tsinghua PBCSF Chief Economists Forum

palgrave
macmillan

Editor
Jiandong Ju
PBC School of Finance
Tsinghua University
Beijing, China

ISBN 978-981-97-0205-3 ISBN 978-981-97-0206-0 (eBook)
https://doi.org/10.1007/978-981-97-0206-0

This Palgrave Macmillan imprint is published by the registered company Springer Nature Singapore Pte Ltd.
The registered company address is: 152 Beach Road, #21-01/04 Gateway East, Singapore 189721, Singapore

Paper in this product is recyclable.

Introduction

Tsinghua PBCSF Chief Economist Forum is held annually in the PBC School of Finance at Tsinghua University, hosted by the Center for International Finance and Economics Research (CIFER). The 2023 forum was held on May 6, 2023, in Tsinghua University. Nineteen leading scholars and chief economists were invited to speak in the forum. Over 5 million audiences attended the forum online. The Forum remained to be the highest level of economic forum with the largest audience in China.

The main theme of the forum is **2023 Global Financial Turbulence and Economic Outlook**, including a keynote speech and dialogue focusing on the theme of **global financial turbulence and changes in the world order**, and three roundtables focusing on China Economic Outlook, Global Financial Turbulence and China's Financial Market, and Global Financial Turbulence and China's Economic Outlook, respectively.

This collection of speeches reflects views on the main economic and financial issues in China and the world from leading experts mainly inside China. Readers can see that these views are different, and some of them may be very different from the views outside China, especially from the United States and Europe. Readers can also see that experts have divergent opinions on many issues. Therefore, this book continues to play an important role in showing how leading experts inside China view the Chinese and global economy and finance.

I would like to thank Professor Liangfei Gu, Chairperson of the School Council of PBC School of Finance, Tsinghua University, for supporting this forum. I thank research fellows at CIFER, who helped me in editing this book: Chen HUANG and Yuankun LI helped edit Chapter 1. Lu FENG and Sijia LI helped edit Chapter 2. Mengyu WANG and Yujia YANG helped edit Chapter 3. Qingtao LI and Sijia LI helped edit Chapter 4. My thanks go to CIFER administration team, Ms. Lvyuan YANG, Ms. Zhiwei XIA, and Ms. La WEI, who worked very hard and efficiently to help me organize the forum. Again, I thank Mr. Jacob DREYER from Palgrave who continues to support this book.

Jiandong Ju
Unigroup Chair Professor at PBC
School of Finance at Tsinghua
University
Director of Center for
International Finance
and Economics Research (CIFER)

Contents

List of Contributors

Tao Guan Global Chief Economist at BOC International (China) CO., LTD

Qifan Huang Former Mayor of Chongqing Municipality

Haizhou Huang Managing Director and Chairman of Capital Market Committee China International Capital Corporation

Jiandong Ju Unigroup Chair Professor at PBC School of Finance in Tsinghua University, Director of Center for International Finance and Economics Research, PBC School of Finance, Tsinghua University

David Daokui Li Director of the Academic Center for Chinese Economic Practice and Thinking (ACCEPT)

Xunlei Li Chief Economist at Zhongtai Securities

Yuanchun Liu President of Shanghai University of Finance and Economics, former Vice President of Renmin University of China, and co-founder of China Macroeconomy Forum

Ting Lu Chief China Economist at Nomura

Wensheng Peng Chief Economist at China International Capital Corporation (CICC)

Stephen Roach Former Chairman of Morgan Stanley Asia, Senior Fellow, Paul Tsai China Center, Yale Law School

Jianguang Shen Chief Economist at JD.com

Xuan Tian Associate Dean and Chair Professor of Finance at PBC School of Finance, Tsinghua University, NPC deputy

Ge Wu Chief Economist at Changjiang Securities

Yang Yao Dean of The National School of Development, Director of China Center for Economic Research, Peking University

Bin Zhang Senior Fellow, Deputy Director at the Institute of World Economics and Politics Chinese Academy of Social Sciences

Xiaoyan Zhang The Xinyuan Chair Professor of Finance and Associate Dean at PBC School of Finance, Tsinghua University

Yandong Zhang The President of CAIJING Think Tank, Managing Editor of CAIJING Magazine

Haibin Zhu Chief China Economist at J.P. Morgan

Min Zhu Vice-Chairman of the China Center for International Economic Exchanges, Former Vice President of the International Monetary Fund

CHAPTER 1

Keynote Speech and Dialogue: Global Financial Turbulence and Changes in the World Order

Abstract In view of the current bilateral economic and trade relations between China and the United States, Stephen Roach believes it is necessary to enhance Sino-US bilateral communication and mutual trust, and jointly address the risk of global recession. Firstly, China and the United States need to rebuild trust, such as by reopening consulates, relaxing visa restrictions, and easing restrictions on non-governmental organizations; secondly, it is important to lower investment barriers between the two countries and reach a consensus on investment protection agreements. Lastly, Roach suggests the establishment of a Sino-US Secretariat, serving as the core of the new diplomatic framework between the two countries, playing a proactive role in the communication and coordination of national affairs. In response to the issue of global financial instability, Min Zhu believes that the banking industry is facing systemic mismatches and the global liquidity crisis will continue to spread. DaoKui Li believes that to maintain and ensure growth, the Chinese government and the market must act simultaneously, and the regulation of artificial intelligence must depend on the coordination and cooperation between China and the United States. Finally, given the backdrop of the current world economic turbulence, Jiandong Ju believes that China should adhere to a nine-(Chinese) character strategy in the competition of great powers: not seeking hegemony, stabilizing the Asian market, and sharing benefits for all.

J. Ju (ed.), *2023 Global Financial Turbulence and Economic Outlook*,
https://doi.org/10.1007/978-981-97-0206-0_1

Keywords Economic growth · Sino-US conflict · US monetary policy · Asian community · Artificial intelligence

1.1 Threading a Needle: Conflict Resolution Amid Recession Risks

Stephen Roach, Former Chairman of Morgan Stanley Asia, Senior Fellow, Paul Tsai China Center, Yale Law School

It is a great honor for me to join this high-level forum. Now, it is Friday evening in Connecticut, and Saturday morning for everyone else. I am a professor at Yale University and a former Chairman of the Asia–Pacific region, and I was also the Chief Economist of Morgan Stanley for 30 years. I think joining the Tsinghua PBCSF Chief Economist Forum is very important, and the discussions on related topics, especially with Chinese experts, American experts, and global experts, are very important.

Today, I would like to talk about the background of global economic challenges, especially the challenges for China and the United States, as well as the conflicts between the two countries.

The convergence of these forces will be very difficult, bringing huge challenges that are hard to cope with for both countries, and at the same time, will have a profound impact on the global economy. Today, I would like to briefly introduce the challenging global macro environment and its impact on the turbulent global financial markets.

First, let's comment on the fragile state of global economic growth. I want to make an important point about the direction of interest rates, and at the same time, I also want to talk about the role of monetary policy in the current environment, as well as a series of unfortunate mistakes made by central bank governors in recent years. This is also a lead-in because I will then talk about the prospects for China's economic growth and its impact on the global economy. The conclusion is to share with you some of my analysis and outlook on the Sino-US conflict, as much of the content is from my newly published book, shown on the right side of the screen, called "Unintended Conflict." Let's start with global economic growth.

This chart shows the ups and downs of the global economy over 50 years. On the one hand, it is very complex; on the other hand, it is also very simple. I hope you will pay attention to the two horizontal lines. The first line is the horizontal black line at 3.5%, which is the trend growth line of the global economy over the past 65 years.

The second line is the red dashed line at 2.5%, which is a threshold line. Below this line, the global economy generally falls into a global recession. The gray area between these two lines, between 2.5 and 3.5, represents what I call the warning zone. When global economic growth falls into this area, it becomes very fragile, lacking a buffer during a dollar shock, otherwise, the global economy would be much stronger. So when shocks come, such as the increasing conflicts in recent times, the world economy will fall into the gray area and often lack resilience, unable to prevent further recession.

As you can see on this chart, in most cases, although not all, when the world economy slides into this area, a global recession occurs, usually within a short period of time.

Finally, what I want to tell everyone is that in this chart, on the right-hand side of the prediction, the predictions and estimates for 2023 and the next 5 years, from 2024 to 2028, come from the latest IMF World Economic Outlook, which was announced a few weeks ago at the IMF's annual meeting. It tells us some very important information, in the next 5 years, in the medium-term future forecast, it is very important to have confidence, the growth from 2024 to 2028, according to the latest IMF forecast, is expected to average only 3.0%, which is the weakest 5-year forecast growth value, according to the data released by the IMF, since 1991. So, not only will the world economic forecast be in the stall warning area but it will also be very weak in the next 5 years, especially in the stall warning area, according to the analysis, the global economic vulnerability will be very serious, especially when facing shocks, which may lead to a global economic recession rate.

The global macroeconomic situation, the long-term decline in long-term interest rates has ended, it is clear that this is the conclusion we can draw from this chart, which shows the actual interest rate of 10-year US Treasury bond yields and nominal yields, which is a forward-looking inflation expectation indicator, produced by the Federal Reserve Bank of Cleveland. In 1982, the long-term world interest rate was 8.4%, and then it began to decline sharply, basically halving in 10 years, to 3.7%. After that, interest rates entered two stages of the Great Moderation, in the first stage, which lasted for about 20 years, from 1992 to mid-2011, the world's long-term interest rate averaged 2.4%. The second stage lasted for 9 years, from pre-pandemic 2011 to 2019, with the world's average interest rate at 0.5%. Of course, during the COVID-19 shock period, the actual long-term interest rate was 0, and recently it has started to rebound, currently at 1.6%, between the lower and upper limits. The question we must answer immediately is, where will interest rates go next? Of course, I will not talk about all the interest rate issues here, I want to explain three reasons why I think long-term interest rates will start to rise from here, roughly returning to the threshold of moderation.

First, global savings are very important, for the decline in interest rates, it will be absorbed, and more and more will be absorbed, especially the growth of spending, in today's world, we are at the beginning of dealing with serious security threats, in China, in the United States, in Europe, in Japan, and South Korea.

The second reason is that we will move from globalization to deglobalization. Conflicts will continue in the coming years, and I will talk about this again later.

The third reason is that, in my view, although inflation has risen a lot since the outbreak of COVID-19, it has now begun to decline, and it is still a very sharp decline. We will not return to the pre-pandemic inflation trajectory. So my conclusion is that the era of long-term inflation has ended. This is the third reason why long-term real interest rates will rise.

The role played by the central bank is very important in promoting the development of the financial market. As everyone knows, I think we are now in such a period, we are in a very unfortunate policy mistake period in history. In this chart, it clearly shows that inflation is rising sharply, and the short-term interest rate as a benchmark for the Federal Reserve is further widening the gap between the two. The Federal Reserve has made a series of mistakes in recent years. The first mistake was to misdiagnose the current inflation as temporary inflation, which is actually the same mistake that I made when I worked at the Federal Reserve in the early 1970s, when the Federal Reserve misdiagnosed many inflationary pressures and also diagnosed it as temporary inflationary pressure in the early 1970s.

Secondly, the Federal Reserve actually realized its mistakes too late, and when it realized that it was correcting them, it did so too quickly. Its speed in correcting mistakes greatly shook the stability of the financial system, leading to the crisis of Silicon Valley Bank. This crisis continued to ferment, eventually causing many large regional banks in the United States to suffer crises. Of course, this also includes the crisis that Credit Suisse experienced. The Federal Reserve made a serious mistake. From a regulatory perspective, it relied on stress tests, which had been very successful since the outbreak of the global financial crisis, but it missed a very obvious point for the Federal Reserve, which is that the design of stress tests involved continuously increasing interest rates and evaluations of enterprises, and the evaluations in the banking sector were missing. The stress tests' practice over the past few years has always focused on interest rate declines, and they did not have enough imagination or creativity to think about what to do if interest rates rise.

Now let's take a look at China. As everyone knows, if you have been following my research over the past few years, I have been very optimistic about China for the past 25 years, but I am now more cautious about China's economic growth. In this chart, you can see that GDP growth in the Chinese economy has accounted for about one-third of the cumulative growth in the global economy over the past 25 years. The black solid line on this chart shows a very sharp decline in the 5-year average of smoothed real GDP growth, which peaked in 2007. The current IMF forecast has already dropped to 4.7% and will drop to 4.7% by 2024, down from 11.7% in 2007. In terms of economic prospects, there is no doubt that I recognize that economic growth will be strong this year. The Chinese government has set an official target of 5%, which will be easily achieved and even exceeded, possibly reaching over 6%, due to the change in COVID-19 policies, economic recovery activities, policy support, support for the real estate sector, and supply chain repair, coupled with a very strong long-term outlook. However, I think if we look further at the growth prospects beyond this year, I think we still need to be cautious. Unlike the past 45 years, the Chinese economy has continuously demonstrated strong and powerful long-term trends over the past 45 years. I now see that this cup is empty, and I am worried about the structural challenges and potential GDP growth, which I will discuss further with you later.

In addition, the impact of turning to President Xi Jinping's thoughts and the conflicts and tensions in geopolitics, as well as the relationship between the United States and China, make me cautious. The potential growth for China's future potential growth, within this framework, there is no secret in the TFP total factor growth rate and growth relationship in this picture. China's working-age population reached its peak in 2016. To maintain strong growth in the economy when reaching its peak, the only way is to accelerate the growth of productivity. However, your TFP is developing in another direction, with a decline of 1.4% on average since 2011. The challenge of population structure has not yet ended, and the working population will continue to decline in the next 10 years. However, if it is possible to offset it, it is to further improve TFP, but in my opinion, this possibility is reduced. The recent weakness of TFP reflects the shift of growth momentum from high-efficiency sectors to low-efficiency state-owned enterprises, which is very important. In my opinion, the challenges of regulatory policies faced by China's private sector, especially the challenges faced by the platform economy, also need our attention.

The story I just told you is not unique to China. We have also seen the same situation in Japan. In the past 30 years, as you know, on the left side of this population structure, Japan's working-age population peaked 18 years earlier than China. On the right side, in 1998, when Japan's working-age population peaked, TFP still fluctuated narrowly and failed to offset the impact of the shrinking working-age population on the Japanese economy. The Japanese economy stagnated, and it has only grown by about 1% in the past 30 years.

Finally, speaking of global macro, I want to emphasize that although many people, including myself, are very concerned about the impact of the Sino-US conflict, we have only recently obtained the impact of long-term conflicts on the macroeconomy, leading to pressure on globalization. The International Monetary Fund released a report, the Global Economic Outlook report, which put forward a very important point and also through some very creative modeling, revisiting the fragmentation of foreign direct investment and dividing it into two camps of the global economy, led by China and led by the United States. According to their estimates, in the long run, the differentiation of foreign direct investment will reduce global output by 2%.

(Lagarde) also quoted a report from the European Central Bank in a recent speech, which studied the impact of supply chain shocks, which also originated from conflicts and de-globalization. The European Central Bank's report emphasized that the impact on costs would lead to higher inflation, with a long-term increase of 1%. Combining these two studies, we can see the prospect of global economic stagflation, lower growth, and higher inflation.

Finally, let's take a look at the Sino-US conflict, which is also the issue analyzed in my recent book. This book not only focuses on the United States and China but also on the relationship between the two countries and proposes that the issue of the relationship between the two countries has become a systemic issue, which is generally based on the wrong narrative of the United States about China and China's wrong narrative about the United States. Such relationship issues also require relational solutions.

In the United States, the political consensus is that the United States has a China problem. When I went to China in March to attend the high-level development forum, I also heard that the consensus in China is that China has a US problem. I disagree with both of these, and I think we both have a common concern about the issue of our bilateral relationship.

The conclusion of this book is that there are three suggestions to resolve conflicts, which are also based on my diagnosis of relationships. The first is to rebuild trust, which is easier said than done, but there are some small steps, which are also written in the agenda, such as reopening consulates, relaxing visa restrictions, reopening educational exchanges, and relaxing restrictions on non-governmental organizations to rebuild trust at the civil society level.

Then there are some more difficult issues, and if we want to cooperate on these issues, they are very important, including climate change, global health, and cybersecurity. This is an ambitious agenda, and my suggestion is to start with the simple and take it step by step.

The second point is to reduce investment barriers, including those between the two countries, and to reach an agreement on bilateral investment protection agreements. Both countries are very active in supporting bilateral investment protection agreements, and we were close to reaching an agreement in 2016. We need to return to the negotiating table to conclude these negotiations.

The third and final suggestion, which I strongly advocate, especially in the current situation, is that the two countries have no substantive contact. Therefore, I propose the establishment of a China-US Secretariat as the core of a new contact structure. It should be a full-time institution, located in a neutral country like Switzerland or Singapore, with full-time collaborative staff provided by both China and the United States. They can coordinate research based on common data, and the China-US Secretariat has the power to convene and invite experts to solve difficult problems. For example, in the case of the outbreak of

COVID-19, the Secretariat would have the ability to solve problems, so that during a crisis, one country's minister would not call another country's minister and not be answered, as happened on February 4th during the balloon incident. The Secretariat also has the ability to monitor and focus on compliance, especially the implementation of new agreements, with a transparent dispute resolution mechanism.

This is my view of the world and my solution to the conflict between the two countries. This solution is not perfect, but it is at least a solution. The global economic situation and the state of China-US conflict require us to think about solutions, not just focus on problems, so I also end my speech with hope and hand it back to the moderator.

1.2 2023: Global Financial Risks Are Rising

Min Zhu, Vice-Chairman of the China Center for International Economic Exchanges, Former Vice President of the International Monetary Fund

Hello everyone, thank you for the invitation to the conference. I am very happy to participate in this forum and discuss the economic and financial situation with you. I apologize for not being in Beijing due to a temporary business trip. I can only make a pre-recorded video to briefly report my observations of the world economy and finance. I have a PPT, and I will bring it up first.

The topic I want to talk about today is very simple because we are discussing the entire economy and finance forum. The global financial risks are rising in 2023, which is what we have seen recently and a phenomenon that needs attention and importance. We have recently seen turbulence in British and American bank stocks, with Credit Suisse's stock price falling 85% (in red) and Silicon Valley Bank falling 100% (in green). The US bank index has fallen by more than 20% compared to others. European bank stocks have also experienced a significant decline, although there have been some rebounds.

The turbulence in bank stocks and the subsequent fluctuations in Silicon Valley Bank, Credit Suisse, and especially the recent First Republic Bank are related, so this still requires our attention and great concern.

I mentioned in my speech at the China Development Forum on March 25th that the incident at Silicon Valley Bank itself is not a systemic risk, but the nature of Silicon Valley Bank is a systemic risk. Why do I say that?

It is because one of the important reasons for the bankruptcy of Silicon Valley Bank is poor management, poor supervision, and of course, it is related to the mismatch of its balance sheet. The mismatch is mainly due to its holding of many US bonds. When interest rates were very low, as the Federal Reserve rapidly raised interest rates, the total assets underwent significant changes. Therefore, looking at Silicon Valley Bank as a whole, this is an analysis of all US banks, with the bonds held by banks accounting for more than 20% of the entire banking market, which has recently declined to around 25%.

This is divided into two parts: most interest rates are not reflected on the books, the green color can be sold at any time, and the assets will be changed according to the market valuation. As everyone knows, Silicon Valley Bank faced an $800 million valuation loss on the first day, which caused significant problems and directly impacted the capital. Everyone can see that the AFS part is still significant, which is the deferred loss, and the other is the current loss, accounting for 25% of the bank's assets, which has a significant impact. At the same time, as everyone knows, modern technology, especially online banking withdrawals, and the spread of Tweets have a significant impact on bank stock prices, which is very interesting. The spread of Tweets has both negative and positive effects on Silicon Valley Bank, withdrawals are all electronic through mobile phones, and the stock price keeps falling.

Today, a bank problem can occur very quickly. Silicon Valley Bank's bankruptcy in just three days shows that under the influence of technology, media, and communication, a banking crisis can spread rapidly, and these are lessons that need to be learned. The Federal Reserve's liquidity risk has risen sharply, and the lending window has exceeded that of 2008, with a large number of funds, deposits of small and medium-sized banks, regional banks, and ordinary people withdrawing their money under this influence and investing it in money market funds. This is a significant change, and banks have started to tighten loans, causing market liquidity and corporate capital turnover problems. Everyone can see that banks are going down, which is all due to tightened liquidity, and this is happening in the United States even more severely than in Europe. The blue color represents expectations, the gray color represents the impact of funding sources, and the yellow color represents the rapid increase in risk expectations, which also suddenly produced a systemic impact.

Under these circumstances, the CDS interest rate in the United States has soared, reaching the level of 2012, and it has now reached this level. The soaring CDS indicates that the liquidity shortage has put tremendous pressure on the market, so we need to pay attention to this and is still a very important aspect.

Why does this situation occur? Why do I emphasize at the China Development Forum that this is a systemic risk? This is related to the asset-liability structure of the entire financial industry today. The big background is the large expansion of the global central bank's balance sheet. The expansion in 2008 and 2009, from the perspective of the Federal Reserve, was from one trillion US dollars to two trillion, doubling, and the global increase was from around four trillion in 2008 to just over six trillion. As you can see in today's situation, the long-term loose monetary policy after 2008 and the magnitude of the loosening in 2020 are not the same as in 2008. This wave can be seen here, so it suddenly brought the central bank's balance sheet, the scale of the world's ten major central banks, to 24 trillion US dollars, six times the 4 trillion at that time, which is unimaginable. It is because of fiscal expansion, monetization of fiscal expansion, and the continuous fiscal expansion and monetization due to the epidemic, a large number of bonds have been issued, so the bonds held by financial institutions have increased significantly.

You can see this is the Federal Reserve's balance sheet, the green one, and the blue one is the European Central Bank's balance sheet. This is Japan's, Japan's continuous central bank balance sheet expansion, the rapid expansion of the central bank's balance sheet, and low-interest rates. Where did the money go? If it was 6 trillion compared to 2008, now it's 24 trillion, where did the 10 trillion funds go before the 2020 epidemic? It went to various financial institutions, especially becoming the bank's balance sheet.

Due to the long-term easing and supply-side fluctuations, the total demand for inflation generated under the stimulus of easing policies, the Federal Reserve raised interest rates by 500 basis points in a year, which was the rate hike in 2016, and in 1994 it was just over 20, and recently it has increased to 5 to 5.25. So you can see the intensity of this rate hike. During this period, it is difficult for financial institutions to adjust the structure of the government bond assets they have bought in the past years at zero interest rates.

The European Central Bank is also like this, raising interest rates very rapidly, with negative interest rates in 2011, around 2 in 2005, and continuing to raise interest rates now. In such a short period, financial institutions need to adjust their balance sheets and be caught off guard. If you want to maintain more flexibility, you will face current losses, which is a particularly big challenge and pressure for financial institutions, especially banks.

If we look at the existing small and medium-sized banks, regional banks, and the entire assets greater than 500 billion and between 100 and 500 billion, the proportion of uninsured resident deposits, the bankruptcy of Silicon Valley Bank is not without reason, the highest proportion is uninsured. At the same time, once it goes bankrupt, the core capital of 11% is lost at once, and of course, it goes bankrupt. You can see that this is the First Republic Bank, these are high-risk banks, and their deposits are not insured because they have to pay this cost, which is a market behavior, which forces the US Treasury and US regulators to guarantee resident deposits, and the resident deposit insurance system is broken, which is another big thing.

At the same time, we can see that if there are problems with these institutions with deposit insurance of less than 50%, it will cause overall fiscal and systemic liquidity tension and fiscal tension because the government will eventually have to pay the bill, as it stands now. This is not a small number; this is another systemic risk. You have to look at the cost of the rescue if you want to rescue, the cost is very high, and this is a very big pressure on banks and regulators and the current characteristics of the Treasury Department. Meanwhile, even if HTM is not implemented, the impact on Tier 1 capital is significant. According to statistics analyzing all banks in the United States, the worst-performing 20% of banks in the United States would experience a capital loss of 700 basis points. Usually, about 11 percentage points, half of the capital is gone, and the impact is significant. Europe must have a percentage point, yellow for Europe, blue for Japan, and the new economy is also affected because a large amount of US dollars flowed into new economy countries during the dollar easing period, and these countries hold a large amount of US dollar bonds. The mismatch of bank balance sheets is a systemic and widespread problem. Slightly better intermediate banks in the United States will also experience a 3-percentage point change, which will be better in Europe and new economy countries. The impact of systemic mismatches is significant.

Lending by institutions like the Federal Reserve is on the rise, and global liquidity is becoming tight. This gap is huge because it is a mismatch of bank balance sheets. The United States is already the fourth bank, and if it continues to expand, the government's bailout exposure will be significant. This is a recent study by the International Monetary Fund, which is a traditional chart of financial risk liquidity.

Sovereign debt liquidity is starting to tighten, spreads are rising, and returns are plummeting due to valuation changes. The corporate bond market is changing due to the holding of equity debt and changes in corporate operating conditions, causing the corporate bond market to change. As you can see in red, this has led to changes in the stock market, which is also starting to show red. The recent red phenomenon is the most severe liquidity tightening since 2010. We have observed that the crisis of the fourth bank (West Pacific Bank) is happening. Fundamentally, this is a mismatch of bank balance sheets, so it is difficult to repair quickly in the short term. This crisis will continue, and the pressure on market liquidity will continue to increase. To what extent will it form a financial crisis? It will spread to small and medium-sized banks' structural system crises or impact the entire financial system. This is something we need to pay close attention to in 2023.

I give a brief report on this point at today's meeting. Please give your valuable opinions. Thank you.

1.3 To Strive for Steady Economic Growth and Maintain Growth, the Government and the Market Should Make Efforts at the Same Time

David Daokui LI, Director of the Academic Center for Chinese Economic Practice and Thinking (ACCEPT), Tsinghua University

Respected Mayor Huang, respected Professor Gu, distinguished guests, good morning everyone! Today is a good day, May 6th, the World Health Organization announced the end of the global public health emergency, and we can now hold offline events in full compliance with regulations. At this time, we should encourage ourselves, as it has not been easy to fight the epidemic for three years. The speeches just now were excellent, and I highly agree. I will make some supplementary remarks.

My core view is that the current major risks in the world economy and finance lie mainly in China and the United States because the two countries account for 43% of global GDP. The United States is the current center of the economy and finance and the main issuer of international currency. China has contributed to more than one-third of global growth every year on average since 2001. If China and the United States each handle their own affairs well, our actual economy and finances will be stable. At the same time, China and the United States should stand at the height of humanity and do a great job. If this great job is done well, our human affairs will be easier to handle in the future. The main issue in China, the core issue, is to maintain stable growth and ensure growth. This is the core of our future development. As I just mentioned, this is very important for the whole world. One-third of the growth is in China. Our goal is to basically achieve modernization by 2035 and reach the level of a moderately developed country. If this case works, we need an average annual growth rate of 4.6%. Mr. Roach spoke very well. From 2009 to 2019, our average annual growth rate decreased by 0.43. According to this trend, we will fall below 4.6% growth rate in less than three years. Therefore, striving for economic growth and maintaining stable growth is the norm for our future work. This is my simple view.

How can we strive for economic growth and maintain stable growth? To put it in a highly summarized and simple way, we must return to the relationship between the government and the market economy. To be more specific, the government should first do its own job well while nurturing and regulating the market. To be even more specific, there are several things that China's economy must do to maintain stable growth in the coming years. In the short term, we must recognize that the economy is still somewhat cold. Although our tourism industry recovered well in May, and some economic indicators seem good at the moment, there are some indicators that we should pay great attention to. These indicators are generally quite accurate. If we look at the consumer price index and the industrial product price index, we know that both of them are currently very small. The CPI is slightly above zero, just a little bit, less than 1%, and below 0.5. The PPI is -2.5%. These indicators show that our economy is somewhat cold. What should we do? In the short term, we need to provide some appropriate assistance to our consumers. In the past, when consumption was cold, we would immediately turn to infrastructure construction. However, after many years of infrastructure construction, the overall space for infrastructure is not that large anymore. Of course, some areas still need it. What should we do? We should appropriately maintain consumer confidence. I just returned from a week-long research trip in Shanghai two weeks ago. Shanghai has a very good practice that can be promoted nationwide. Shanghai has carefully studied and allocated 1 billion yuan to subsidize consumers in the payment process. No matter whether you are buying a car or clothing, they will subsidize you through the UnionPay process. With just 1 billion yuan, their research found a 1:4 relationship. For every 1 yuan of subsidy, it can stimulate 4 yuan of consumption. What is the concept of 1:4? Your 1 billion yuan is about 4 billion yuan. In terms of the whole country, since our tax revenue is a circulation tax, think about the 4 billion yuan increase in circulation and economic activity. At least 30% is tax revenue, which is 1.2 billion yuan. In the end, fiscal revenue will increase. This calculation should be done nationwide, with the central government promoting local governments to do the same. Of course, this is not a long-term solution, but a short-term measure to maintain consumer confidence.

Second, we must cultivate new markets. There is a major market, a 10 trillion market that could be cultivated, which is the carbon market. Currently, the dual-carbon efforts are carried out independently by various local governments and industries, which goes against economic laws. Why? Let me give a small example: it is absurd for the steel industry to reduce carbon emissions. Why? Because it should be a national strategy, steel production might need to increase, while cement production should decrease. This is because cement used in construction is non-recyclable, and its carbon emissions are high. However, high-speed rail is recyclable. So, how do we calculate this? It is impossible for humans to do it; we must have a carbon market. The market is a supercomputer. As long as we add a little carbon tax to appropriate places, such as crude oil and coal, and gradually increase it, as long as we announce a plan to increase it, many people will automatically calculate it. Coal producers will have to calculate how much carbon tax they need to pay, and coal-using enterprises will have to calculate how much their future coal-burning costs will increase, including coal and cement. How much can be recycled from waste steel? This will automatically start. If the carbon market can be launched, a large number of investments, many green investments, will become profitable. Many entrepreneurs and investors will flock to it. This matter is urgent and must be done. To some extent, it can also improve our public finance through carbon taxes.

The third issue is the flexible retirement system. This year, 2023, those born in 1963 are turning 60, and there are 30 million of them. Within the next five years, according to the current retirement age, nearly 150 million labor force will retire. From paying taxes to social security, how should this be handled? Forcing people not to retire is unreasonable. We need a flexible retirement system. If you are willing to work longer, your pension will be higher. If you want to retire on time, you can receive the current pension. This reform must be in place. After careful calculations, we believe that Mr. Roach's earlier statement is slightly pessimistic. Indeed, China's population is declining, but considering the population quality, education level, and public health level, our human resources are rising and will continue to rise until 2050. The key is how to make good use of our human resources. We believe that flexible retirement is very important. I found that many world-class companies do this. Leaders and management retire on time, but engineers and R&D personnel can work as they please. If you have experience, you can continue to work. This is very pragmatic. Speaking of the Chinese economy, we calculated that if these reforms are in place, the potential growth rate from 2020 to 2030 is 5.9%, which is still relatively high. So why is our inflation so low now? Why is it negative growth? It's because we haven't reached our potential growth rate. In the next decade, from 2030 to 2040, its 4.9%, which is still quite high. This is China's issue. We must do a good job in growth, and the government and the market must work together. The government must do its job, start the market, cultivate the market, and correct the market.

What is the issue with the United States? The United States needs to address one thing: financial stability. There is no need to worry about the growth of the United States, as it still has vitality. A recent figure revealed that non-farm employment in April increased by 290,000. The United States still has growth potential, innovation potential, and vitality. The key issue is financial instability. The biggest risk is not short term; the biggest risk is losing faith in the US dollar. Can people still trust the US dollar after rounds of turmoil? The crux of the matter is the international currency status of the US dollar. How can the United States achieve financial stability? It must also find answers in the relationship between the government and the market economy. There are two issues that have not been resolved, and the Americans are well aware of them, but they are difficult to change. The first issue is more direct: financial supervision. Why has there been a financial crisis or panic every 12 years since 1978? The actual problem lies in financial supervision. Simply put, the cat that catches mice cannot catch up with the mice. The supervisory authorities are not as capable as the financial innovation institutions. Everyone knows that the smartest finance students in the United States go to Wall Street, the second-tier becomes lawyers, and only then do they go to financial regulatory agencies. It is a complete inversion of ability, round after round. Why is there an inversion of ability? To a large extent, the financial regulatory system is highly fragmented, and it is difficult to form highly professional and honorable institutions. For example, in the case of banks, there is a department in the US Treasury that supervises national banks, while state banks have some people supervising them. Silicon Valley banks are regulated by California. The supervision is highly fragmented. Listed companies are regulated by the SEC, while unlisted companies are decentralized. The Federal Reserve has admitted that there is a problem with their supervision. They admitted that there was a problem with the supervision of such an important bank as Silicon Valley Bank and that they need to reflect on it. The United States must solve the problem of the cat not being able to catch the mice under financial supervision and should appropriately centralize it.

The second question is, why can't the United States maintain financial stability? This is a bigger and more difficult question. The budget, the worst part of American democracy, has turned the federal budget into a competition arena for local politicians. The United States has also discussed many times the need to transfer power from Congress to an independent structure. Frankly speaking, the United States manages monetary policy better than fiscal policy. The Federal Reserve is independent, but the budget management is not. The next major issue is whether the debt ceiling can be raised before June 1st. If it cannot be raised, another round similar to the 2011 financial panic will occur, which is a completely suicidal behavior. This has become a mechanism for the Republican Party to fight among themselves.

I just mentioned that the United States must fundamentally reform and reflect on its roots. This may sound like a tall tale, but how can the United States listen to China? The American intellectuals are also reflecting. Blinken recently spoke at the Brookings Institution in the United States, saying that we need to reflect on our system and learn from China's experience.

Finally, for the world to be stable, China and the United States must work together on one absolutely important issue, which I believe is more important than managing the economy. It is the new "nuclear weapon" of our time—artificial intelligence. No one can clearly see the long-term impact of artificial intelligence on humanity, and opinions are not unified. However, no one can completely deny that artificial intelligence could have a devastating and disastrous impact on humanity. Since no one can rule out this risk, I think it is greater than the risk of climate change. China and the United States are the most important countries in artificial intelligence, with the three most important aspects being computing power, the number of programmers, and big data. Both China and the United States are leading countries in these areas, so the development of artificial intelligence is mainly between these two countries. However, China and the United States must negotiate and sign an artificial intelligence constitution, similar to the nuclear weapons agreements of the past, to define what can and cannot be done and strictly limit the prohibited actions. I believe this is more important than current international politics and geopolitics, and it is a responsibility to humanity. China and the United States should reach a consensus on this issue.

In summary, as the world's major countries, China and the United States, which account for 43% of the global economy, have important responsibilities. Each should focus on its own important issues: China should maintain stable growth, and the United States should ensure financial stability. China and the United States should cooperate in researching and formulating a global human artificial intelligence constitution.

Thank you, everyone.

1.4 Nine (Chinese) Words Strategy in Great Power Competitions: Not Seeking Hegemony, Stabilizing Asian Market, Sharing for All

Jiandong Ju, Unigroup Chair Professor at PBC School of Finance in Tsinghua University, Director of Center for International Finance and Economics Research, PBC School of Finance, Tsinghua University

Thank you, Professor Daokui, for your suggestions. We will discuss them with Mr. Stephen Roach later. Chairman Mao taught us that because we serve the people, we are not afraid of criticism and correction from others. No matter who points out our shortcomings, we will correct them as long as they are correct. If your suggestions are beneficial to the people, we will follow them. Following Chairman Mao's teachings, I will also share some preliminary views on great power competition. Please criticize and correct me.

My view on great power competition can be summarized in nine words: not seeking hegemony, stabilizing Asian market, and sharing for all. Let me explain. First, I need to clarify that this is a personal academic discussion and does not represent any organization. It is open to criticism, discussion, and correction.

The nine-word strategy.

Not seeking hegemony means not pursuing global domination. Why? I think there are three reasons: it's not feasible, it's not beneficial, and it's not appropriate.

Stabilizing the market, what does that mean? It means economies closely connected to China's market should establish an Asian Community. We know that the rules of the WTO, fair, transparent, free, and non-discriminatory trade are almost non-existent now, and China cannot promote WTO rules globally. However, we can restore WTO rules of fair, transparent, free, and non-discriminatory trade within the Asian Community. How to do that, exchange markets for rules. In the past few decades, we have exchanged markets for technology. I think we should change our approach now and exchange markets for rules. How do we exchange markets for rules? China will unilaterally open up to members of the Asian Community that abide by WTO rules, lowering tariffs to zero. You can enjoy China's market, but you must follow WTO rules.

What means sharing for all? That means market sharing, knowledge sharing, technology sharing, opportunity sharing, and development sharing, especially technology sharing. Professor Dao Kui just mentioned that AI technology should be shared. How can it be shared? I will discuss this in detail later.

First, let's talk about not seeking hegemony. According to the International Monetary Fund's estimates, China's GDP surpassed the United States in terms of purchasing power parity in 2016. If we consider nominal GDP, by 2022, China accounts for 18% of the world's GDP, while the United States accounts for 25%. Dao Kui and his team have made detailed calculations. If China's GDP maintains a growth rate of 4% to 6% in the next 10 years, China's nominal GDP will surpass the United States between 2030 and 2040, becoming the world's largest economy. According to the Organization for Economic Cooperation and Development's forecast, by 2060, China, India, the United States, and the European Union will be the world's first, second, third, and fourth largest economies. The GDP shares of these four economies will be approximately 26% for China, 18% for India, 15% for the United States, and 12% for the European Union.

Due to the pressure of population decline, China's share of the world's GDP will peak between 2050 and 2060. Combining these data, we can make two predictions. First, after 2035, China's GDP will remain the world's largest economy for a long time. Second, China's share of the world's GDP will not exceed 30%, and the combined GDP of any two of the second, third, and fourth largest economies will surpass China.

Looking back, there have been two major hegemonic countries in the past: the United States and the United Kingdom. When the United States established its global hegemony in 1945, its GDP accounted for 53% of the world's GDP. In 1860, the United Kingdom's industry accounted for more than 50% of the global industry. Our conclusion is that with a 30% share of the world's GDP, China's economic size is not sufficient to seek global hegemony. Therefore, based on this data, we draw three conclusions: it's not feasible for China to seek hegemony because the market power is not sufficient to dominate, and the cost of seeking global hegemony is greater than the benefits. It's inappropriate because, as we have seen, the 21st-century world economic structure will feature long-term competition and coexistence between the United States, China, India, and others, not supporting any country's global hegemony, neither the United States nor China.

How can we understand the changes in the current world order? The current situation is a paradigm shift in the world order. What is a paradigm shift? From 1500 to 2018, the world order paradigm was the iteration of hegemony, starting with Spain and Portugal, followed by the Netherlands, France, Britain, and the United States, with new world hegemony constantly iterating. However, after 2018, the paradigm of the world order changed, becoming a world order of competitive coexistence. How can we understand such a paradigm shift? Since the 1990s, human capital and innovation have replaced material capital as the main driving force for world development, and human capital is mainly the population with higher education, which is naturally distributed around the world, unlike the financial capital or material capital that can be highly concentrated in a few hegemonic countries.

The GDP share of the top five world economies in 2022 is as follows: the United States 25.41%, China 18%, the European Union 16.61%, Japan 4.22%, and India 3.38%. The strength of the United States can no longer support its world hegemony. As mentioned earlier, the future changes in the world situation are due to the changes in the distribution of human capital in the world. Why will China and India become the world's first and second-largest economies by 2060? The most important reason is population; a large population will become human capital. The populations of China and India are both more than four times that of the United States. When China's GDP per capita reaches a quarter of that of the United States, China's total GDP will surpass the United States. If India's GDP per capita reaches a quarter of that of the United States by 2050, India's GDP will also surpass the United States. Therefore, if the United States wants to maintain its current world hegemony, it must contain China. In 20 years, it will also need to contain India. If the European Union and Russia reconcile, it will also need to contain the European Union and Europe, which is unsustainable.

From this analysis, the disagreement between the United States and China in the world order is that the United States wants to maintain the old hegemonic order, while China wants to adapt to the new competitive coexistence world order. This is the first conclusion.

Where does this disagreement manifest itself? China's second strategy is to stabilize the market. Why is it to stabilize the market? In order to maintain its previous hegemony, the United States' great power competition strategy is manifested in the so-called "small courtyard high wall," de-Sinicizing the high-tech field. In a world without China, isolating China, the United States seeks to maintain its high-tech hegemony in a world where China is isolated. The United States' 2022 Competition Act, Inflation Act, and Chips and Science Act restrict and prohibit trade with China in the high-tech field, protect American technology, contain China's technological innovation, and attempt to lead China by at least 1–2 generations in core high-tech fields.

The United States' technology trade policy clearly violates the WTO principles of "non-discrimination, fairness, transparency, and free trade." We need to pay close attention to this point. Suppose China is de-Sinicized by the United States and subjected to American technology blockades. In that case, China may be oppressed into the domestic market, and eventually, even the domestic market may not be defended, dominated by American-led multinational capital technology monopolies, marginalized, and the global economic structure may return to an American-dominated pattern.

What should China do? I have listed here the top 50 economies with the highest dependence on Chinese trade. Mongolia, Kyrgyzstan, Hong Kong, China, Iran, Australia, South Korea, and Japan are among the top 50. I suggest establishing an "Asian" community, with the term "Asian" in quotes. Among the top 50 countries and regions, in the "Asian" countries and regions with close economic ties to China, we should restore the WTO principles of "non-discrimination, fairness, transparency, and free trade." If the global community cannot agree, we can restore WTO principles within our own closely connected "Asian" community. Bilateral negotiations should proceed from easy to difficult in an orderly manner, exchanging market access for adherence to rules. If you are willing to abide by WTO rules and not discriminate against China in the factor markets, you can become a member of the "Asian" community. In this way, we can establish a "non-discriminatory, fair, transparent, and free trade" technology market. I suggest that the Chinese market can unilaterally open to members of the "Asian" community, and Chinese tariffs can be unilaterally reduced to zero first, with other members reducing their tariffs to zero within a certain period. China's reduction of tariffs to zero will have some costs, but we are willing to bear these costs in exchange for WTO rules and to promote the construction of the "Asian" community in a snowballing manner. First, let's look at Cambodia, Laos, Malaysia, and Vietnam.

Second, the governance of the "Asian" community is dynamic, with the entry and exit of member economies being the norm. If you are willing to abide by WTO rules this year, you can join; if you violate WTO rules next year, you will exit. Countries and enterprises that participate in US chip legislation and other measures to contain China, discriminate against the Chinese market, and violate WTO rules will lose preferential conditions in the Chinese market.

South Korea has recently discussed with the United States whether to abide by US legislation and contain China. I raise three questions:

1. After more than 30 years of diplomatic relations between China and South Korea since 1992, are South Korean enterprises willing to give up the Chinese market, which has grown together with them?
2. Is it in the best interest of South Korean enterprises to participate in containing China's technological innovation?
3. Even if South Korean enterprises participate in containing China's technology, can they really hinder China's technological progress?

Sharing for all: A world order of coexistence and competition is a shared world order, with shared markets, knowledge, technology, opportunities, and development. China, the United States, and Europe need to face issues such as climate change, virus control, nuclear proliferation, war, and peace, as well as the challenges posed by the direction of AI technology development that has already arrived. The core challenge of the AI era, in my opinion, is the interest conflicts between the monopoly of technological elites and the sharing of technology by all humanity. Here, I use the description of the future world by Israeli historian Yuval Harari in his book "Homo Deus," where he suggests that "god-like beings" may emerge, with technological elites controlling algorithms, algorithms controlling robots, and robots controlling ordinary people. Such a scenario is getting closer and closer to us. If this scenario occurs, can the "god-like beings" remain in power forever? No, human society may fall into turmoil for hundreds of years as "god-like beings" will inevitably emerge, be overthrown, and replaced by new "god-like beings" in a cyclical pattern.

So what should we do? AI technology products are natural monopolies, like large models such as Chat GPT, and brain chips have strong characteristics of increasing returns to scale, with huge fixed costs and almost zero marginal costs. Without intervention, the core products of AI will monopolize the global market, with a few technological elites monopolizing the intelligence of the entire human race. Therefore, it is necessary to design a system for the AI era to prevent the monopoly of human intelligence through system design.

How to design a system? Look at these companies, Apple, Microsoft, Amazon, and Tesla, the power of these super companies has already surpassed the strength of medium-sized countries, and only the governments of the United States, China, and the European Union, the three major economic entities, can counterbalance them. Ensuring competition in core products is the minimum requirement for ensuring the healthy development of human society in the AI era. I suggest that there should be at least six companies worldwide for core products such as large models and brain chips, two in the United States, two in China, and two in the European Union. Of course, the more, the better, to ensure a minimum level of competition. The tripartite global governance system of the United States, China, and the European Union is the institutional guarantee for global technology sharing rather than monopoly. Let me stop here.

1.5 Dialogue: Global Financial Turbulence and World Order Transformation

Jiandong Ju, David Daokui Li, Stephen Roach, Live Audience

We have 10 more minutes, and we will have a little more dialogue with Mr. Stephen Roach. Please, Professor Dao Kui.

Jiandong Ju: I think we should first invite Mr. Stephen Roach, the only guest from the United States, to take this rare opportunity to hear his feedback on our speeches.

Jiandong Ju: Stephen, let us know if you have any comments.

Stephen Roach: The previous speeches have raised very important issues. Zhu Min mentioned volatility, which is closely related to my expressed views, that is, the policy decisions of the Federal Reserve and other central banks. Although our statements are different, I think this volatility can be said to be heaven-sent. Li Dao Kui may be more optimistic about China's economy, and you also raised very important points. Although the labor force population in China is declining, the improvement in the quality of the labor force can compensate to some extent. Undoubtedly, China has invested heavily in human capital, especially in the field of education, which could also be a very important compensatory factor. However, I think it is difficult to rely solely on the improvement of labor quality to offset the decline in quantity, especially if government policies continue to support low-productivity state-owned enterprises, and the regulatory environment is full of uncertainties, which will reduce support for the private sector. Therefore, you have indeed raised very important points, especially in terms of measuring growth from a quality perspective.

Finally, the point raised by our host, that is, the Sino-US conflict and great power competition, indeed poses enormous challenges and affect world stability and peace. Personally, I feel that we need to pay more attention to the way the two countries interact, rebuild mutual trust, which is currently lacking. Moreover, I believe that this is also the necessary condition for coexistence that you emphasized. All these speeches are very enlightening, and I am very grateful for everyone's views. Thank you.

Jiandong Ju: Thank you, Stephen, and David.

David Daokui Li: The two issues Jiandong Ju mentioned are very important. One is the "Asian" community. In fact, RCEP has already emerged, with three parts of Asia: the first and largest part being China, the second-largest part being Southeast Asia, and ASEAN. ASEAN, with a population of 600 million, has already formed a unified market. We have already established RCEP with them, so the problem is not significant. Thirdly, Japan and South Korea, as you mentioned, are very important. We must make it clear to them on the issue of chips, and I completely agree with this.

The second small response is about artificial intelligence. The severity of artificial intelligence is even more serious than what you said. It's not just about technical elites ruling the world, but eventually machines ruling the world, and technical elites can't even rule anymore. This issue needs to be clarified. So many technical elites think they can create a machine to rule humans, but in the end, they are ruled by it. This is equivalent to nuclear weapons. The common enemy faced by China and the United States is this. As long as there is a common enemy between China and the United States, many things can be done without being enemies with each other. I believe that the more serious the situation you mentioned, the higher the possibility of cooperation. These are the two comments.

Jiandong Ju: Thank you, Stephen and David. Mr. Roach just mentioned that the first thing needed between China and the United States is to restore trust. To restore trust, for example, we face common challenges. David and Stephen both mentioned several common challenges we face. Everyone knows that climate change is a challenge, nuclear proliferation is a challenge, virus prevention and control is a challenge, and now there are new challenges, such as preventing global financial turmoil, which is very important. In addition, David repeatedly emphasized the challenge of where AI technology is heading for humanity. Such challenges can enable China and the United States to put aside geopolitical conflicts and face the common challenges faced by humanity, promoting the healthy development of human society.

Due to time constraints, our first round of dialogue ends here, and we open the floor for questions.

Question 1: Thank you for the wonderful sharing from the mentors and guests. My question is for Mr. Roach. Can Mr. Roach tell us who he hopes will participate in the China-US Secretariat, and whether this mechanism will be effective in the future, from losing trust to rebuilding trust and other aspects? Thank you.

Question 2: I would like to ask Professor Ju Jiandong, the scope of the Asian community definitely includes a large range from Southeast Asia to Russia to the Middle East and Central Asia. My question is, if we want to draw this scope to the Southeast Asian region, which means that China has a certain concept of establishing an economic community with Southeast Asia, will it bring about a larger backlash from the United States in terms of international politics or geopolitics? This may also be related to some issues in our southeastern region.

Question 3: I would like to ask Professor Li a question. I agree with the China-US Secretariat, the Asian Community, and artificial intelligence. What I am most concerned about now is how China can maintain stable economic growth because this is the current issue, and that is the issue of tomorrow. Now we are facing today's problems, and I hope to hear from Professor Li on how to stimulate market potential and the vitality of private enterprises under the current situation, and what the government should do to cooperate or what it should do. I have seen that recent central meetings have talked about boosting the confidence of private enterprises, how to solve employment, financing problems, market fairness issues, etc., but often many central policies have deviations when they reach the last mile of local implementation. Professor Li must have a lot of research on this aspect, and I hope you can give us some suggestions and ideas in this regard.

Stephen Roach: Regarding the "China-US Secretariat," my new book introduces its functions and governance structure. However, to briefly respond, in my view, the members of this secretariat should largely invite professionals and experts from a wide range of different fields, especially experts in China-US relations, economics, trade, innovation, technology, policy, and so on.

We have actually explored many of these areas today, such as global health, climate, and cyberspace. We can invite experts in these fields, of course, they must be professionals and have a good education. In addition, we can also invite practitioners at the diplomatic level, and the composition of members should be balanced between American and Chinese professionals. In fact, this is just a concept for everyone to think about. I would describe it as a relationship-based think tank, empowering it to assess existing agreements and new agreements to be formulated and to resolve disputes in the implementation of these agreements. But what I want to emphasize is that this is a cooperative institution. I don't think the Chinese team should go it alone, and I can't imagine the American team doing their own thing in such a secretariat. In my view, such a secretariat must be a cooperative platform, dedicated to solving problems, such as writing policies and white papers together, not just written by the Chinese side or the American side.

The Chinese and American member teams are composed of professionals who can work in a neutral space. They work together, go to work in the same building every day, and become more and more familiar with working together. This model can re-establish the cooperative relationship between these professionals and gain trust.

So, there are actually many details about my suggestion, and I just made a supplement. Thank you.

Jiandong Ju: The second question is for me, and I would like to make a few points. First, the WTO rules are considered the most successful and helpful rules for world trade after World War II by all countries, with non-discrimination, free trade, transparency, and fairness. What China demands is only the WTO rules, non-discrimination, and not to discriminate against or contain China. In the long run, this should be supported by all countries. Of course, some countries, such as South Korea mentioned earlier, want to follow the United States to contain China's technology, which will have costs. If they abide by the WTO rules, they can enter the Chinese market; if they do not abide by the WTO rules, they may lose the Chinese market. For example, they cannot enjoy zero tariffs and may suffer from relatively high tariffs. Under such a system design, I think these countries and economies can make choices according to their own rationality and national interests, and it is dynamic. This is the first point I want to make, to provide such an explanation.

Another point, I would like to mention is a past example, such as the Asian Infrastructure Investment Bank (AIIB). At that time, when China started the AIIB, it seemed that not many economies would join, but who was the first to join outside of Asia? The United Kingdom, the UK was the first to join.

David Daokui Li: You asked a very good question about how to achieve stable growth and how to motivate local governments to protect and support the private economy. I would like to share a few thoughts. First, the private sector is the most important part of China's market economy activities. It plays a crucial role in resolving employment issues and promoting local economic growth. Motivating local governments to protect and support the private sector requires leadership from the central government. Under the central government's guidance, local governments at all levels should fully implement the central policies to protect and support the private sector.

Second, private companies commonly face difficulties in financing and borrowing, as well as insufficient liquidity. Our monetary policies and state-owned banks' lending policies could be moderately relaxed to provide funding for private enterprises, resolving their short-term cash flow and financing difficulties.

Third, market development and construction cannot be separated from a stable and reliable business environment and legal system construction. There should be equal treatment of private enterprises, and selective law enforcement and "letting companies prove their own innocence" style supervision should be eliminated.

Finally, public opinion has a significant influence on entrepreneurship and market confidence. We should create a positive public opinion environment, with the central government taking the lead to introduce specific opinions to support private economic development, boost market confidence. Thank you!

Jiandong Ju: Thank you, Professor Li. Due to time constraints, our very exciting discussion will end here. Let's give a warm round of applause once again to thank Mr. Roach and Professor Li.

CHAPTER 2

Roundtable I: China Economic Outlook

Abstract Turning around China's economic issues, the experts at the Roundtable I talk about their own views. **Qifan Huang** believes that there are four aspects of dividends to be released for China's economic growth, i.e. reform dividends, super-large-scale market dividends, innovation and capital market dividends, and new opening-up dividends. So the future prospects of the Chinese economy are bright, and the current difficulties are temporary. **Yang Yao** emphasizes two aspects of the Chinese economy. First, China has taken the lead in some fields of new technologies. Second, after the reform and opening up, the Chinese economy generally has a 10-year cycle, and the 2020s should be a new growth cycle. From these two perspectives, Yao Yang believes that the Chinese economy is in a new growth cycle. **Yuanchun Liu** points out that the economic data for the first quarter showed a series of conflicts, which shows that supply and demand are not synchronized in the recovery. He thinks this is a new stage, with new characteristics, new logic, and a greater need for new policies. **Xuan Tian** thinks that in the short term, we rely on consumption; in the long term, we rely on innovation; and from beginning to end, we rely on the private economy. The direction of reform is marketization, legalization, and internationalization.

Keywords Future technology · New growth cycle · Scale · Proactive fiscal policy · Rebound · Employment

J. Ju (ed.), *2023 Global Financial Turbulence and Economic Outlook*,
https://doi.org/10.1007/978-981-97-0206-0_2

2.1 China's Economy Stabilizes and Looks Forward to a Bright Future

Qifan Huang, Former Mayor of Chongqing Municipality

Leaders, experts: I am very happy to participate in today's roundtable forum. The Central Political Bureau meeting on April 28 conducted an in-depth analysis of the current economic situation and made comprehensive arrangements for the next step. I am full of confidence in the Chinese economy as I deeply study the spirit of the 20th National Congress and the Political Bureau meeting. I believe four aspects of dividends are to be released for China's economic growth.

First, organically combining supply-side structural reform with the strategy of expanding domestic demand to release reform dividends.

The 20th National Congress of the Communist Party of China emphasized the need to organically combine the implementation of the strategy to expand domestic demand with deepening supply-side structural reforms. Since the reform and opening up, China has formed the world's largest and most growth-oriented middle and high-income groups. China currently has over 400 million people with an annual household income of 100,000–500,000 yuan and a large-scale high-income group. The demand of these middle and high-income groups is mainly reflected in the consumption upgrade of mid-and-high-end products and services. Even during the epidemic in the past few years, while they could not go out, consumption of tourism, studying abroad, and shopping mostly stayed in the country, and the total amount of imported high-end brands did not decrease. According to Bain statistics, the global personal luxury goods market shrank by 23% to 217 billion euros in 2020, the first market contraction since 2009. However, during the same period, China's personal luxury goods market showed a counter-cyclical growth. In 2020, the scale of China's personal luxury goods market reached 346 billion yuan, a significant year-on-year increase of 47.9%. Moreover, Chinese consumers' preferences and Chinese elements are becoming the main considerations for international brands in formulating marketing and design strategies. The so-called "consumption demand supported by income" mainly focuses on this group of people.

In fact, China's macroeconomic operation has been plagued by insufficient total demand for a long time, and insufficient domestic demand is a superficial phenomenon. To a large extent, it is due to the existence of many supply restraining policies in the fields of mid-to-high-end products and services in China, which leads to limited growth in supply capacity and thus fails to fully release the huge effective demand with payment capacity. To effectively expand the consumption of middle and high-income groups, gradually drive employment, and use employment to drive more employment, thereby increasing the income of other groups and promoting the economic cycle to gradually enter a new level of dynamic adaptation of supply and demand. This is also the essence of building a new development pattern with the domestic cycle as the main body and the mutual promotion of the dual cycle.

For example, China's annual automobile sales have exceeded 27 million units for more than five years. Although the market scale has ranked first in the world, car ownership per thousand people is only more than 200 units, which is basically at the bottom among countries with similar income levels in the world. Behind this are a large number of restrictions on driving, license plates, purchases, and lagging construction of parking buildings and road networks, which have suppressed automobile consumption demand. Sorting out these two aspects can effectively stimulate automobile consumption. According to China's current growth rate, car ownership per thousand people has the potential to reach more than 400 units in the next ten years, and the annual sales volume has the potential to increase by 10 million units, reaching more than 37 million units. There are many similar industries and fields, such as demand for improved housing consumption, personalized high-quality medical, health, education services, low-altitude aviation, boats, racing cars, horse racing, other types of consumption demand, etc. The main reason why these areas have not developed is the existence of a large number of supply-restraining policies, which should be released through deepening supply-side structural reforms to release these effective demands and promote high-quality economic development with new reform dividends.

Second, creating an tremendous unified market to release market dividends.

Entering a new stage of development, the Chinese economy will welcome a new dividend after the labor dividend—this is the dividend generated by our super-large-scale single market, namely the market dividend. In terms of scale, China has a population of 1.411 billion, accounting for nearly 18% of the world's total population. In terms of market structure, China is a single large market. A single market refers to a market with a unified legal system, tax system, business rules, and language and culture. In terms of industrial foundation, China is an economic entity with all-factor, full-category, and full-industrial chain integration. The combination of these three factors will produce a scale economy effect. For manufacturing industries entering the Chinese market, once the scale is achieved, six costs can be significantly reduced: the R&D cost, the fixed asset investment cost, the procurement cost, the labor cost, the logistics cost, and the market development cost. Generally speaking, the scale economy can affect 30–40% of the total manufacturing cost, and once a sufficient scale is reached, the price can be reduced by about 30–40% to defeat foreign competitors with a price advantage.

This scale economy effect is a new dividend naturally generated by China's development to this stage, and it is also the natural logic contained in the Chinese-style modernization with a huge population scale. Driven by this large market, the logical layout of multinational companies' industrial chains is sales-in-the-location-of-production and production-in-the-location-of-sales. Sales-in-the location-of-production means using the local comprehensive factor cost advantage to organize production and sell to the global market. The cost-sharing effect of China's large market will be an important factor affecting multinational companies' "in China, for the world" strategy. Production-in-the-location-of-sales means organizing production for the local market and better organizing the supply chain to respond to changes in consumer demand, that is, "in China, for China." China's 1.4 billion population market will be a huge "gravitational field." This is also the origin of the confidence in stabilizing our foreign trade and foreign investment base.

Third, constantly opening up new fields and new tracks, and releasing talent innovation dividends and capital market dividends.

First is the talent and innovation dividend. Constantly opening up new fields and winning new tracks is an effective means to adapt to the requirements of the new technological revolution, to break various decoupling and disconnection schemes, and to seek technological self-reliance and self-strengthening in the new situation. On the one hand, the Chinese economy has the conditions and capabilities to continuously open up new fields of development and win new tracks. From the demand side, China has become the world's largest online retail market and is about to become the world's largest consumer market, and this market is constantly upgrading and updating, which will provide fertile soil for local innovation.

From the supply side, China has a large-scale talent pool and engineering team and a market entity group that can industrialize various creative innovations at any time, which is also an important source of China's increasing innovation confidence and momentum. In 2020, the population with a university education in China reached nearly 220 million. According to the sixth population census, from 2000 to 2020, the number of people with a university education per 100,000 people has risen from 8,930 to 15,467, and China has trained 60 million engineers in the last 20 years. The World Intellectual Property Organization's Global Innovation Index ranking shows that China has risen from 34th in 2012 to 11th in 2022. With China's super-large-scale single market, full-industrial chain manufacturing advantages, and talent advantages, as long as there is a little "spark" of innovation, it can create a new blue ocean of industry with a "prairie fire" momentum, and in turn provide a broad space and stage for technology application, technology integration, and technology iteration. This is the huge talent and innovation advantage of the Chinese economy. We must transform these potential advantages into real advantages through a new round of deepening reforms, making them the talent and innovation dividends that promote the high-quality development of the Chinese economy.

Second, the capital market dividend. How to play the supporting role of the capital market in the development of the national economy is the key to deepening the reform of the basic system of the capital market, connecting the whole chain of innovation with the reform of the capital market, and the high-level closed loop of technology-finance-industry, which is the key to building a new development pattern. At present, the registration system has been implemented. But to achieve the long-term stability of the capital market, a series of basic system reforms are still needed.

I think there are at least two aspects: first, improving the delisting system. The success of the registration system requires coordination with the delisting system. We cannot continuously approve listings on one side while some zombie companies cannot be delisted on the other side. By the end of 2022, there were 5,079 listed companies in China. In the future, the implementation of the registration system and the improvement of the delisting system will achieve a roughly balanced number of initial public offerings and delistings, so as not to drive out good money with bad money. Second, we need to promote the entry of long-term funds into the market. We should further expand the proportion of social insurance funds, including various types of pension funds, entering the market to provide sufficient financial support for the continuous and stable development of the capital market. It is suggested to further promote the enterprise annuity system and improve the investment system of enterprise annuities. There are at least three benefits: (1) Improving the investor structure and the management of enterprise annuities will inevitably give birth to a group of institutional investors; (2) With the development of enterprises, enterprise annuities will become larger and larger, providing a continuous source of funds for the capital market, and promoting the capital market to enter a virtuous growth track; (3) It helps to connect ordinary employees to participate in the capital market and obtain property income channels.

Fourth, promote the implementation of RCEP and release new opening-up dividends.

The 20th National Congress of the Communist Party of China has systematically deployed to promote a high level of opening up to the outside world. At present, a key task of opening up is to promote the implementation of RCEP and release a new round of opening-up dividends through high-level introduction and going out. There are five specific aspects:

First, the rules of goods trade promote the development of related industries. Taking agricultural products as an example, the proportion of zero-tariff products exported from China to Japan has increased significantly from 20% to about 60%, and the opening of agricultural products between China and South Korea and ASEAN has also exceeded the existing bilateral free trade agreements. These measures provide convenience for China's agricultural product exports and also help to expand the import options of other countries' advantageous agricultural products. In addition, RCEP's trade facilitation measures also provide institutional guarantees for the rapid clearance of fresh agricultural products.

Second, the threshold for access to service trade is reduced, and the demand for services will increase significantly. For a long time, China's huge volume of goods trade has not played the driving advantage it should have for the development of service trade. RCEP member countries have reached market access commitments in service trade that exceed the current level of openness. The expansion of trade and investment activities brought about by RCEP will inevitably lead to the expansion of the supporting service chain, which objectively provides good conditions for China to develop digital trade, intellectual property services, R&D

and design services, cross-border logistics, and other productive service industries, as well as life services, cultural services, and tourism services.

Thirdly, the in-depth application of the rules of origin brings four major benefits to China's industrial development: the new rules of origin within the entire RCEP scope effectively lower the threshold for enjoying preferential tariffs, driving the expansion of the overall trade scale within the region. In order to meet the rules of origin standards, enterprises will use more intermediate products with the region for production, which helps to further deepen the division of labor within the region and optimize the industrial chain layout. It attracts multinational companies outside the region to increase their investment in the RCEP region in order to fully enjoy the benefit of rules of origin. It is conducive to the development of small and medium-sized enterprises, which can fully utilize the upstream supply chain within the region, overcome their own disadvantages of limited individual value-added, increase the regional value component of their products, and thus more easily meet the rules of origin standards and enjoy the tariff preferences of the agreement.

Fourthly, it is conducive to high-quality introduction and accelerates the formation of internationally competitive industrial chain clusters. By further opening up the domestic market with the help of RCEP, China can better attract foreign investment and multinational enterprises to continue to gather the industrial chain, supply chain, and value chain of manufacturing, especially the core links, in China, and accelerate to promote the expansion and cluster of these chains.

Fifthly, it is conducive to high-quality going out and promoting the construction of the "Belt and Road." The implementation of RCEP will significantly enhance the level of economic integration in East Asia, optimize the business environment within the region, and thus enhance the trade creation effect brought by free trade agreements, promote the integration of industrial chains, supply chains, and value chains within the region, promote the free flow of factors, strengthen division and cooperation, expand and upgrade the regional consumer market, and promote the further development of regional industrial chains and supply chains, which is of great significance for the economic recovery of East Asia and even the world.

In conclusion, the future prospects of the Chinese economy are bright, and the current difficulties are temporary. As long as we unswervingly deepen reform and opening up, unswervingly promote high-quality development, and continuously release the dividends of reform, market, talent, innovation, and opening up, we will be able to maintain China's economic growth rate at above 5%. We should have full confidence in this! Thank you, everyone!

2.2 Dialogue with Qifan Huang

Yandong Zhang, Qifan Huang

Yandong Zhang: Thank you very much, Mayor Huang, for analyzing the new dividends, including the reform dividend, the large market dividend, the productivity growth dividend, the innovation and capital market dividend, and the new opening-up dividend. In the new opening-up dividend, you mentioned a point that our trade pattern has changed. I would like to ask a question: now some of our enterprises are moving their factories to Southeast Asia, how do you view this issue?

Qifan Huang: Because we have reached the RCEP agreement with Southeast Asia, there is a rule of origin agreement in it. As long as any of the more than ten countries increase the value-added of the processing by 20%, it is considered as a product of that country. In this way, when exporting in world trade, it can become a tariff-free product. In recent years, the United States, under Trump and Biden, has imposed tariffs on us and engaged in trade frictions, treating China unfairly. The RCEP has hedged against this issue. If our exports are subject to a 30% tariff, but if the products are placed in Southeast Asia, as long as there is a 20% increase in the final processing, it is considered a local origin and is not subject to any tariff pressure from Europe and America. In this sense, the RCEP rules of origin have become a very powerful weapon for the Asian region to deal with US trade friction and tariff conflicts. This is one aspect.

Secondly, the labor force in Southeast Asia is now much cheaper than that in coastal China, about one-third of our current labor costs. Therefore, moving some labor-intensive production, light industrial textile processing, or electronic assembly tasks to Southeast Asia is actually beneficial for enterprises. If you look into the foreign investment in Southeast Asia in recent years, it has grown a lot, with 60% of the foreign investment coming from Chinese enterprises, not European and American enterprises. It may seem like these enterprises have no confidence in their own country and are moving abroad, but in fact, it is the credit effect of RCEP that has deeply influenced our private enterprises and various enterprises. This is a manifestation of everyone making full use of the policy.

As I just mentioned, many of our enterprises have moved their processing to Southeast Asia and then exported their products. However, the components, raw materials, and upstream and downstream resources of these products are still in mainland China. As a result, the trade volume between mainland China and Southeast Asia has increased from over 600 billion US dollars to 900 billion US dollars. This reflects that, in the long run, this is beneficial for both China and Southeast Asia. It is a consequence of resource allocation and implementation of RCEP policy. In this sense, for China, it is better to strengthen, expand, and supplement the weak links in our current industrial chain clusters, and better develop new products in our industrial chain clusters. If you develop it yourself, who will arrange the industrial chain layout? It is the leading enterprises, chain-leading enterprises, or manufacturing core enterprises that arrange the layout. If you lack core enterprises, lack leading enterprises in processing, and lack chain-leading enterprises like Apple, you will not be the boss of the industrial chain layout. You are just taking advantage of the advantages of production and sales. But if we have production and sales, large industrial chain clusters with leading enterprises, and the abilities of inventing and creating new products, we will truly master the initiative of the industrial chain layout. In the future, we can arrange the industrial chain clusters in China or abroad according to the production and sales conditions of foreign countries. This is the scenario that the Chinese manufacturing industry should have in the future.

Yandong Zhang: Thank you very much. Thank you, Mayor Huang. His point is that letting the peacock fly southeast is a good thing for China.

2.3 China's Economic Outlook

(**Moderator: Yandong Zhang**, The President of CAIJING Think Tank, Managing Editor of CAIJING Magazine.

Speakers: Yuanchun Liu, President of Shanghai University of Finance and Economics, former Vice President of Renmin University of China, and co-founder of China Macroeconomy Forum, **Yang Yao**, Dean of The National School of Development, Director of China Center for Economic Research, Peking University, **Xuan Tian**, Associate Dean and Chair

Professor of Finance at PBC School of Finance, Tsinghua University, NPC deputy)

Yandong Zhang: Now let's invite our three guests to the stage. One is Yuanchun Liu, President of Shanghai University of Finance and Economics and Co-founder of China Macroeconomic Forum (CMF); another is Yang Yao, Professor and Dean of Peking University's National School of Development and Director of China Center for Economic Research; and the third is Xuan Tian, Chair Professor and Associate Dean of Tsinghua University's PBC School of Finance. Please welcome them.

I apologize to the three professors, as we are running short on time. In the first round, each person will speak for 6–7 minutes. I'll start with Professor Yang Yao.

Professor Yang Yao recently proposed a new cycle concept for the Chinese economy. How do you explain your new cycle?

Yang Yao: Good morning, everyone! I believe the Chinese economy is in a new growth cycle, which can be understood from two aspects. On one hand, from the perspective of the long cycle of technology, you may have noticed that there is a view among foreign, especially American economists, that the whole world has entered a stage of long-term stagnation. However, in the past 5 or 6 years, we have seen new technologies constantly emerging, and this time China has taken the lead in the field of new technologies. For example, China has a significant advantage in the technology fields with many applications, such as AI, new energy, new energy vehicles, biotechnology, etc. China is firmly in the first camp, even dominating. Regarding AI, its more extensive application is in automation, not only ChatGPT. In this regard, China is definitely leading the world with the most industrial robots. If you look at the automation management of cities, the so-called smart city management is beyond our imagination. New energy is even more self-evident, and China's advantage over the rest of the world can be described as overwhelming. As for new energy vehicles, the only competitor to China seems to be Tesla, and it would be tough for other traditional car companies to catch up.

In some future technology areas, China is definitely not lagging behind and is firmly in the world's first camp, such as quantum computing, quantum communication, nuclear fusion, photonic chips, etc. When we hear about nuclear fusion, we think of the highest energy output achieved by the United States, which was widely circulated on the Internet at the time. In fact, China has the longest duration in the world, 403S or 405S, but it is not widely reported domestically. In fact, this is a great achievement, and China is not lagging behind in these fields. Therefore, in the new round of technology cycles, China is at least in the first camp, if not leading, which is very important.

The second aspect is the cyclical issue of the Chinese economy itself. After the reform and opening up, the Chinese economy generally has a 10-year cycle: high growth in the 1980s, adjustment in the 1990s, ultra-high growth in the first decade of the new century, and adjustment after 2010. If this cycle holds, we should see that we have entered the 2020s, which should be a new growth cycle. Moreover, during the last adjustment, we have firmly established a concept, which is to move from virtual to real, and the real economy has become the goal pursued by every enterprise, and complicated technology has become the goal pursued by our enterprises. So, from these two perspectives, we have entered a new growth cycle.

Yandong Zhang: Thank you very much. In fact, the new cycle you mentioned is driven by technology. Chinese technology is already at the forefront of the world. As far as I know, China is cooperating with France in nuclear fusion, which is different from the United States. The United States uses laser ignition. From a technical point of view, I asked the former president of the Chinese Academy of Sciences, Chunli Bai, who said that there is still a long way to go from an application perspective. However, American technology does have some ignition and energy generation, which China does not have, but its duration is very short. So, from an overall perspective, I am curious to know how the scientific community views whether we have reached the forefront. This is a question. In addition, I also noticed that you mentioned the scale issue of China's manufacturing industry. From a scale perspective, China's scale is definitely large, but is a large scale necessarily strong? We certainly hope that China's technology will be at the forefront, but I don't know if it is so optimistic. Professor Yang Yao, what do you think?

Yang Yao: I am still quite optimistic. Not to mention those technologies that have not yet been applied, such as quantum computing and nuclear fusion, China already has massive advantages in the application field, like the new energy vehicle field. As we just mentioned, it may take decades for nuclear fusion to be commercialized. During this transition period, what do we use when fossil fuels are no longer viable? It is solar energy because wind energy is too scarce. The primary source is still solar energy. China has an overwhelming advantage in the field of solar energy, not 100%, but at least a crushing advantage. We firmly occupy this, and the leading technology is in our hands.

New energy vehicles may destroy the entire fuel vehicle market. China is firmly in the first camp in the field of new energy vehicles and is far ahead. The latest data shows that NIO ET7 sales in Germany have already surpassed BMW 3, the best-selling model in Germany. Moreover, Germans are starting to accept Chinese electric vehicles. It cannot be said that China leads the world in all fields, but we can see that at least in the visible wave of technological innovation or application, China occupies a leading position.

Yandong Zhang: Technology-driven is very important for the next round. Thank you, I will ask more later. President Liu, what do you think? It seems that you have proposed a new stage for the Chinese economy. How is this new stage defined? What kind of stage is it? Thank you.

Yuanchun Liu: We need to discuss some perspectives here. The discussion just now was very macro, and the historical perspective can be extended to the Kondratiev cycles, which can only be understood by discussing things at least 50 years apart. Of course, I agree with Mayor Huang's view that China has huge dividends, and we must not be pessimistic about China in the medium and long term, especially as Professor Yao Yang also mentioned our technology. In fact, it is essential here to see the trend rather than the absolute level. That is, our patents did not surpass the United States, and our highly cited papers did not surpass the United States, but in the past three years, we have surpassed them. Although we do not surpass the United States in some leading industries, we have already surpassed the United States in several industries, which attracted the attention of Americans, especially with the emergence of the neck-choking problem. The emergence of the neck-choking problem does not mean that our technology is lagging but can be recognized as the result of our rapid and challenging progress.

Therefore, in the historical context of the Sino-US conflict, facing the suppression of the United States, our first reaction should not be pessimism. In fact, this is the result of our progress and changing the pattern. Therefore, in the face of such a conflict between challenges and responses, we should hold a relatively optimistic attitude. I think this is an optimistic view in the long run as challengers.

Yandong Zhang: We need to look at the trend.

Yuanchun Liu: Yes, in the short term, we will see that if we want to make ourselves stable and go far, we must take every step well, not walk while looking at the horizon or fly while looking at the Big Dipper, which may cause problems. Therefore, if we focus on the present, we will find that we have many problems. These problems are further focused on the fact that Politburo mentioned that the recovery's foundation still needs to be stable, but I believe that China's recovery has entered a new stage. There is a significant disagreement in this new stage because the data for the first quarter showed a series of conflicts, such as our three major demands are rising, the money supply is still high, but our prices are falling. For example, our market expectations are very poor, but our foreign trade growth rate and foreign capital growth rate are higher than expected. We see that the current "May Day," "Qingming," and "Spring Festival" travel index has shown a retaliatory change, and our companies seem to be unprofitable, with profits declining rapidly. We have always talked about our proactive fiscal policy, but in fact, everyone will find that in the first quarter, general public expenditure plus fund-based public expenditure, year-on-year growth is basically zero, not as we imagined, with the government report showing that the annual fiscal expenditure and broad fiscal expenditure budget reached about 7%. What went wrong here?

We saw that the real estate data for February and March were very good, but the transaction data for April suddenly dropped. Everyone is also wondering if there will be a cold snap after the small spring. In addition, we saw the "May Day phenomenon" and the "Zibo phenomenon," but the total tourism ticket revenue reached only 84% in 2019. Here, we will see very conflicting data, leading us to draw different conclusions based on different data interpretations. It precisely confirms that our recovery has entered a new stage after the post-epidemic restart, a stage we have not faced before, requiring us to rethink and grasp its operational logic, then make corresponding adjustments based on this logic.

Let me give you the simplest example: why is consumption up 4.6%, investment up 5.1%, exports up 14.8%, and the price level still falling? It's simple because demand is rising fast, but supply is recovering faster, and demand is not outpacing supply. In general, supply and demand are not synchronized in the recovery, but this cannot be explained as a minor issue.

For example, we see a retaliatory rebound, with year-on-year data looking good but very poor year-on-year profit data. Our retaliatory rebound is in travel data, the recovery of social interactions, and the restoration of transaction orders, not the recovery of profits. So the first stage of recovery is social repair, but it has yet to transition to profit repair and balance sheet repair, let alone the expansion phase of our balance sheet. Therefore, we will see that our focus on macro analysis is not only on our "three engines" but, more importantly, on the matching between supply and demand and, at a deeper level, the repair of the balance sheets of the four major economic entities, as well as the adjustment and mutation of behavior during this repair process. Therefore, based on such logic, we should analyze the performance of different departments at the central and local levels under the drive of fiscal support and the endogenous motivation of the new concept of political achievements. This may lead to a good analysis and understanding of our current economic situation and the next steps in our action plan.

I think it is a new stage, with new characteristics, new logic, and a greater need for new policies.

Yandong Zhang: I am very inspired. President Liu talked about social repair rather than profit and balance sheet repair, so this economic recovery is actually a complex mix of various extreme and different factors, which also brings some difficulties to our policy decision-makers. It is not one-way thinking but multi-dimensional or non-linear thinking. Which breakthrough do you think is better from the policy level? Thank you.

Yuanchun Liu: The current mutation of many data is normal but needs more professional analysis. For example, we need to clearly understand the differences between month-on-month and year-on-year data and distinguish well between compensatory recovery and conventional recovery, or there will be some policy object errors. That is, if you misunderstand, the logic will be wrong. This is the first point I want to make.

Secondly, we need to pay close attention to the underlying logic of some of our current policy implementations, which is to say, what kind of model our fiscal policy should adopt under the current challenging fiscal repair, especially the challenging local fiscal repair. We must use proactive fiscal policies to truly achieve positive effects. First of all, your expenditure must reach a speed of 5–6% and remain stable, which is very important.

Another critical point is that the current M2 is very high, and the new loans of 10.6 trillion have basically set a new historical high. However, a large amount of credit liquidity is circulating within the financial system, simply circulating among the government, banks, and state-owned enterprises. If we want the current monetary policy to penetrate the microeconomic unit, especially private enterprises, we must correct some "distortions" in the current monetary policy. This "distortion" is reflected in interest rates. The current policy interest rate is more than 3%, and the medium and long-term loans we give to state-owned enterprises have already fallen below 1.8%. The actual average financing cost of some county-level platform companies and private enterprises may still be in the range of 6–10%. The larger the gap, the more severe the distortion of the entire monetary policy. When we simply use quantitative injections and structural injections, it brings about the circulation of money and the distortion of interest rate policies. Therefore, the profits of state-owned enterprises are currently outstanding, with a year-on-year growth of more than 9% in the first quarter. However, private enterprises are at a financial loss, especially small and medium-sized ones.

Why is this happening? You will find that its financing costs and various environments have remained the same but have become even worse. How can monetary policy change such a situation? Our traditional thinking is that fiscal policy digs holes, and monetary policy releases water. But who does the fiscal policy dig holes for? It digs holes for state-owned enterprises. Therefore, the recovery of large and state-owned enterprises is very rapid and pleasing, but private enterprises have no movement. Our explanation for the lack of motivation and confidence in private enterprises is incorrect. We participate in many activities of entrepreneurs, and large state-owned enterprises, private enterprises, and big capitalists may lack confidence, and they have concerns indeed. However, small and medium-sized entrepreneurs are still eager to change the loss pattern, and the younger generation still has full feelings for the motherland.

Here, we will find that for the so-called problem of insufficient confidence in private enterprises, we have gone about several tasks at a time without stratified processing and stratified correspondence and have not made targeted policy adjustments for different types of enterprises. Changing some of our traditional ways of coordinating fiscal and credit policies is essential. For state-owned enterprises and state-led project financing costs are so low, and the gap between our policy interest rates is getting bigger and bigger, should we moderately reduce policy interest rates and reduce such a mismatched "distortion"? It is very important, and I think it is the most important.

The second important point, which we should also pay great attention to, is that although the price level has not entered the deflationary stage at present, the decline in the month-on-month and year-on-year prices will definitely hinder the recovery of profits. Therefore, how to prevent the decline of the price level has been given many suggestions by Politburo, which is to expand domestic demand and reverse people's confidence. In this regard, we still need some new thinking on policy points rather than sticking to traditional consumption policies. We must genuinely investigate the hotspots of residents' consumption. I have discussed a simple point on many occasions: we have now reached the second and third cycles of "decoration." Can we provide a new round of "decoration" subsidies for the people instead of simply using traditional policy tools?

For example, we have been talking about affordable housing for many years. Why can't we accelerate the urbanization process of our citizens through affordable housing and release the consumption dividends of migrant workers during the urbanization process? So, we need some new ideas here.

Of course, there are also international issues that everyone talks about. I think the most important thing is that when the global economy is very sluggish, China must quickly recover and play the role of a super-large market economy, using its profit space and market space to break the strategic layout of the "small courtyard high wall" just formed by the United States. This is an urgent matter. The current international and domestic environment in the new stage puts forward higher requirements for our grasp of policies, requiring us to have a broader vision in our thinking. I won't go into details.

Yandong Zhang: Thank you very much. You talked about monetary policy, fiscal policy, and domestic demand. In your recent articles, you mentioned domestic demand is a driving force. Now I would like to ask Professor Tian to share some thoughts on short-term boosting consumption in domestic demand.

Xuan Tian: Today's theme is the outlook for the Chinese economy. The GDP growth rate has been waving from the epidemic to the present, 6.1 in 2019, 2.2 in 2020, and 8.4 in 2021, with an average of 5.3. From 6.1 to 5.3, it has dropped a step. Last year it was 3%, and this year's government work report set it at around 5%. Many people are optimistic, thinking it could reach 5.5 or even 6. Even if we reach 6, last year was 3, and this year is 6, averaging 4.5, which is still a step-down. Compared to the previous two years, 5.3 has dropped another step. The first quarter has passed, and the data is alright, 4.5, exceeding expectations. The Central Political Bureau meeting also said that the three pressures are easing. However, in the long run, if our country's economy returns to the potential growth rate, the essential point is that it relies on consumption in the short term and on innovation in the long term. But the important means throughout is the private economy. These are my basic view.

Why rely on consumption in the short term? As Professor Daokui Li just mentioned, I actually went to Shanghai for research two weeks ago, specifically looking at how to stimulate or boost consumption. Objectively speaking, consumption is an important means to improve in the short term. In the first quarter, GDP was 4.5, and consumption contributed 3 percentage points, accounting for two-thirds of economic growth. When we went there, we felt that the impulse to communicate, dine, gather, and travel, which the epidemic had suppressed for three years, had indeed been released. However, when we looked at the data carefully, it had not yet returned to pre-epidemic levels.

For example, during this year's May Day holiday, everyone felt that there were huge crowds everywhere, with a reported 274 million trips made. What do these 274 million trips mean? Going to three tourist attractions counts as three trips, so some people estimate that about 50–60 million people travel during the May Day holiday. Our tourism revenue reached 150 billion, comparable to the 100% level in 2019. I think this is a very high EQ statement. What does 100% actually represent? In fact, airfares and admission fees are rising, which means that the number of trips is increasing, but consumption is not increasing, and the money spent by ordinary people is decreasing. What does this actually represent? It means that our consumption has not really returned to the pre-pandemic track. Many viewers or students may say they see everyone going out to play in their friends' circles, with huge crowds, and even going to Zibo for a barbecue. The last time they went to Zibo was during the Spring and Autumn Period and the Warring States Period when the Five Nations attacked Qi. To all the viewers, including those watching the forum, you are not really experiencing the rise in consumption. In other words, our consumption is very unbalanced. 50–60 million people traveled during the May Day holiday, but in fact, there are 1.4 billion people in China. According to our statistics, 1 billion people have never taken a plane. What does this represent? It means that we are a polarized society, and what we see in our friends' circles is not the same as real life. Do we have delivery guys, housekeepers, or cleaning ladies in our friends' circles? Most of us don't. When we look back at our consumption, there is an increase, but there is no natural rebound, retaliatory rebound, or a very balanced rebound.

What do we rely on to boost consumption in the short term? It mainly depends on income, as consumption is a function of income. At the same time, economic theory tells us that income is not a short-term boost to consumption. It's not that getting an extra 500 yuan bonus this month can change my consumption habits. What is the most important factor in changing our consumption habits? In fact, it is our long-term income. So, what does long-term income depend on? Going back to what we said earlier, it depends on employment. Employment represents a stable cash flow. If I have a job, I will have a stable expectation for the future and enhance such a mindset.

Yandong Zhang: So, I want to ask if consumption can be boosted in the short term.

XuanTian: I want to say that in the short term, we need to develop our economy by boosting consumption, but it doesn't mean that consumption can be boosted in the short term. What does consumption rely on? It relies on increasing income, and income ultimately depends on employment. Employment is actually a very important indicator. The data for the first quarter seems okay, but we see structural employment. For example, a very important data point is the unemployment rate for those aged 18–24, which is 19.6%. This number is relatively high and is already very close to 19.9%, which existed last year when the epidemic was most severe. Moreover, employment is cyclical, and we haven't reached the employment season yet. Now it's April and May, and this number will be even higher by July. It's a pity if a student, after 6 years of primary school, 6 years of middle school, and 4 years of college, cannot find a stable job after more than a decade. What does boosting employment rely on? It mainly relies on the private economy. We are all familiar with 5, 6, 7, 8, and 9 figures: more than 50% of a country's tax revenue comes from the private economy, more than 60% of GDP, more than 70% of innovation, 80% of employment, and even 90% of the number of enterprises rely on the contributions of private entrepreneurs. If we go to the southeast coast, to Jiangsu, Zhejiang, and Shanghai, these numbers are even close to 6, 7, 8, 9, and 10, and they always rely on the private economy. A very important issue for the private economy is the lack of confidence of private entrepreneurs. Everyone has been talking about boosting the confidence of private entrepreneurs and stabilizing their expectations. Why is the confidence of private entrepreneurs insufficient? It is crucial to handle the market and government relationship, which has always been discussed.

For example, during this year's Two Sessions, the "two unwavering" and "three unchanged" principles were once again emphasized, which sends a significant signal to the market: we still consider the private economy as our own and need to be reassured. I looked it up, and the "two unwavering" principles were first proposed at the Third Plenary Session of the 11th Central Committee in 1978, which I think was a significant theoretical advancement at the time. The "three unchanged" principles were first emphasized on March 4, 2016, during the joint group meeting of the members of the Democratic Construction and the All-China Federation of Industry and Commerce at the Fourth Session of the 12th National Committee of the Chinese People's Political Consultative Conference. So, stabilizing the confidence of the private economy is actually very, very important, which is to handle the relationship between the government and the market well.

I'll just say this much for now: in the short term, we rely on consumption; in the long term, we rely on innovation; and from beginning to end, we rely on the private economy. I only talked about the short term.

Yandong Zhang: I would like to ask Professor Yang Yao, who has been discussing the issue of domestic demand at the financial index release conference for a long time. I think you have done a lot of research on domestic demand, the private economy, and consumption. Can you share your views?

Yang Yao: I've been saying this for three years, and I completely agree with Professor Xuan Tian's statement. In the short term, there is no other way to stimulate consumption. Our country has spent more energy on the supply side in the past three years to fight the epidemic, and of course, there is a reason for focusing on the supply side, which is to protect market entities, and that is also important. However, if demand does not rise, protecting market entities will not work, which is also the cause of the problem mentioned by Professor Yuanchun Liu just now. We are now open, and the economy is recovering and growing, but you find that prices are not rising. Why aren't prices rising? Supply is still there because of many market entities, but demand has yet to rise. For all countries, there is no other way to boost consumption in the short term other than giving people money. There is no other way. If you want people to consume, they must have money first. If income does not grow for three years, people will not consume. If the future outlook is poor, people will consume even less. Other countries have adopted this method, which is to discover gold. Now that this matter has passed anyway, the World Health

Organization announced yesterday that the epidemic is over, and I guess there is no need to mention the discovery of gold. However, consumption this year will not be too bad, and a growth of 6% or 7% is not a big problem. By next year, it will gradually return to the track before the epidemic, and annual growth of 7% or 8% is still expected.

Yandong Zhang: Professor Tian, you have done a lot of research on innovation, and mentioned at this meeting that we need technological innovation in the long run. Can you talk about the combination of technology and industry? How to transform technology and industry into productivity and integrate capital into it? Can you talk about your views on this? Thank you.

Xuan Tian: The question is excellent. Following the previous discussion, relying on consumption in the short term and innovation in the long term, we have talked a lot about technological innovation. We have achieved great success over the past 45 years of reform and opening up. It is very important that we have made adjustments to the original system, which released a lot of productivity. Now we see that if we want to go further and the economy leaps to another level, it depends more on innovation, which is technological innovation.

As for innovation, the main body of innovation is actually enterprises, in other words, private entrepreneurs. As mentioned earlier, more than 70% of innovation relies on private entrepreneurs. For example, universities are also engaged in innovation, and our university scholars are researching more out of interest and spontaneous exploration, which is different from the innovation of enterprises or the main body of innovation. Companies innovate, not innovating for innovation's sake, but driven by profits. We also know that innovation is challenging, which means creating something out of nothing, a process from zero to one.

Mayor Huang also mentioned just now that many innovations in our country are buying in and digesting, from one to infinity, rather than disruptive innovations from zero to one. If we want to make disruptive innovations from zero to one, we need to encourage these entrepreneurs. How to do it? One very important point I still need to finish is that we need to handle the relationship between the government and the market well.

In April, the Central Committee for Deepening Reform mentioned a direction that it is necessary to support the main body of enterprise innovation. What should the government do? We should establish good rules, such as where the boundaries and red lines are, and let the market play a core role in resource allocation to ensure that the main innovation body has a free exploration space. Therefore, a relaxed market environment is crucial for innovation because innovation is an exploration of unknown paths with many trial-and-error processes. If we are intolerant of failure, if the environment is not relaxed enough, it is likely to lead entrepreneurs to focus more on short-term investment rather than long-term innovation.

It is important to properly define the boundaries between the market and the government to determine where we should let the invisible hand of the market play a role and where the visible hand of the government can. This issue is a global challenge. I studied and worked in the United States for over a decade, and I find it also a problematic issue. When I returned to China, I saw that our country has been exploring the boundaries between the government and the market. We need to avoid a situation where the regulatory authorities or the government become increasingly focused on micro-level issues while entrepreneurs become more focused on macro-level issues. Because it has a detrimental effect on long-term innovation for micro-level entities or business entities. Therefore, from the perspective of innovation, we need to provide a good market environment, properly handle the relationship between the government and the market, and encourage private entrepreneurs to make long-term investments.

Yandong Zhang: Now, there is a paradox. In fact, everyone knows that private enterprises' private investment is relatively low. When we conducted research in Suzhou, many entrepreneurs said they would keep the money instead of investing because they could not see the direction clearly. The paradox is that innovation requires investment even if the situation of enterprises is not very good. How to solve this contradiction? This is very realistic in today's China. Most abroad innovation comes from enterprises, and their proportion is relatively high. How can we solve this problem in China now?

Xuan Tian: I will answer from two perspectives. First, from the macro-government standpoint, why do entrepreneurs lack confidence or have unstable expectations for the future? We may need to ensure policy continuity, consistency, and stability. It is important, not just a casual statement, but based on our collaborated paper published in top academic journals using more than 40 countries' data. The conclusion is a country's policies actually have little impact on businesses. Why? Because entrepreneurs are brilliant, they can adjust their investment decisions to adapt to national macro policies. Whether the policy is slightly more capital-oriented or labor-oriented, more proactive or conservative, it doesn't matter. Entrepreneurs can adjust, but what is the most important? It is the instability of policies. In other words, when our market entrepreneurs do not know whether the future will be more capital-oriented, labor-oriented, left-leaning or right-leaning, what they can do is wait and watch. So a fundamental logic is that, objectively speaking, macro policies play a very important role in micro-market entities and business operations. In previous years, everyone mentioned TMT because the market was very hot. However, after encountering problems, the country said that we should invest in complicated technology, we should turn around, and we should strive for a high level of self-reliance. The market immediately followed suit with complicated technology, chips, new energy, new materials, etc. Therefore, the macro guidance of the country plays a very important role in micro enterprises. So what we need to do is to ensure the stability of the country's macro policies. We cannot change them very often. Local adjustments are fine, but stability is the most important. In this way, you can form a continuous and stable expectation for the market, and they can make long-term investments. When the reform and opening up began, it was said that this policy would remain the same for 100 years. What is the concept of 100 years? The logic is that as long as we live, this policy will not change, and we can just do it. It is very suitable for the important characteristics of our so-called innovation cycle, which is very long and the initial investment being very large. This is the first part of the answer to your question.

Secondly, as for how enterprises should operate now, this is also my research and something I have been advocating: to engage in strategic investment and corporate venture capital (CVC). Enterprises face various problems through their own endogenous R&D, so it is better to invest the money in some early-stage projects in the fields they are optimistic about, and then make corresponding investments, cultivate them, and let them grow slowly. When they grow up slowly, I will acquire them and bring their technology and team into my company. It can stimulate innovation because large enterprises never do disruptive innovations. Disruptive innovations are always done by those very small, high growth, adventurous, and entrepreneurial small and micro enterprises. Engaging in strategic and early-stage CVC investment is very important for large enterprises to improve their innovation level. Many international companies, such as Intel, Google, Microsoft, General Motors, and Oracle, and domestic companies, like Huawei, Xiaomi, and BAT, are all engaged in

CVC. However, these companies are at the forefront, and many domestic listed companies and medium sized enterprises have not realized the importance of early-stage strategic investment. In fact, this early-stage strategic investment is a win–win situation. What is a win–win situation? It means that listed companies can make strategic layouts in advance, and allow funds to sink into the real economy simultaneously, enabling these small and micro enterprises to obtain funds and solve the problems of complex and expensive financing.

Yandong Zhang: There is one last question for all the speakers. Everyone may think that domestic demand and consumption are quite important now, and they are also important levers for driving the economy. However, this falls into a paradox. When the common people have worries about the future, they need the state's public fiscal expenditure to invest in people's livelihood. Now, as you mentioned earlier, the state's fiscal policy has contracted. How can this problem be solved? Only when the common people have no worries about the future can they spend money boldly, and this worry needs to be guaranteed by the state. How can this problem be solved?

Yuanchun Liu: I think this question hits the nail on the head. Everyone is talking about principles and common sense, expanding domestic demand, promoting consumption, and stabilizing investment. The catchy slogans are easy to talk about, but actually doing things may not be that simple. I believe many current dilemmas are not simple short-term problems but medium-term problems, not simple policy inputs but institutional reforms. As Mayor Huang mentioned earlier, an important part of the dividends is that we need to build several major dividends for the future, all of which will be based on a new round of major reforms. For example, expanding consumption is an important source of our social infrastructure reconstruction, safety net reconstruction, and major reforms in income distribution policies. It is crucial to break the global income distribution polarization problem.

The second important issue is that the world is facing sluggish growth and high debt. It is also a problem we still need to solve. On the one hand, there is a proactive government, and on the other hand, there is a debt problem accumulated by the proactive government. How to balance these two? At present, the reform of government functions, the optimization of our entire fiscal and taxation system, and the adjustment of the fiscal system are imminent. Therefore, everyone will see that the 20th National Congress focuses on the construction of a modern market system, with eight major aspects, finance being one aspect, and fiscal policy being a very important aspect. But the core, I think, is still in fiscal policy because the pivot of China's socialist market economy with Chinese characteristics is still the government, and the boundary and function division between the market and the government still lies in the reform of the government.

If we do not have a medium-term perspective on the design of some systems, we will definitely fall into a dilemma. For example, the issue of land finance is a huge problem. To break through land finance's dilemma, it needs to reform and reposition the central and local fiscal functions, and the government needs to balance the between industrial investment and social construction, not only the simple return of real estate function. In this regard, I think we need to have a broader perspective and deal with short-term issues which is also an important balance mentioned in the economic work conference.

We must open the curtain of this major reform this year and next year, and bring up some of the issues that everyone is concerned about rather than avoiding them, and we must not cover up some medium-term issues due to the short-term pressures we are facing. There must be a medium-term positioning. So, talking about consumption alone is not the answer, talking about investment alone is not the answer, and talking about expanding domestic demand alone is not the answer. It has several major balances, and I have just briefly mentioned these.

Yandong Zhang: Thank you. Having a medium and long-term perspective and the ability to solve short-term and practical problems, how do you see this, Professor Yao?

Yang Yao: Just now, we talked about the limited consumer methods. Standing in China's current special situation, I am still willing to talk about two points that may work in the short term. One is the issue of the automobile industry mentioned by Mayor Huang. There is still great potential in our country's automobile industry. I have also made a preliminary calculation myself, and I think it is not a big problem for our automobile sales to reach a peak of 40 million units. We are now at 30 million units, and there is still a lot of room for growth.

As Mayor Huang said, all our cities are implementing purchase restrictions, which is completely unnecessary, especially for new energy vehicles. Since everyone is using new energy vehicles, why do we still need to restrict purchases? You can adopt some measures, such as encouraging people to drive less. In fact, this is the case in foreign countries. For example, we can charge a congestion fee, like Singapore and London.

In Beijing, you can charge a fee for entering the third ring road. Adopt this method, do not restrict people's purchases, and follow the trend of new energy vehicles. If the purchase restrictions can be widely lifted, automobile sales will surge.

Another point is real estate. Real estate prices are still falling, but the decline is narrowing. Although our real estate is one of the pillar industries, it has been recognized now. However, the measures we use to solve the real estate decline still need to be improved. At present, local governments are trying to maintain the delivery of buildings, and the government is making great efforts. Of course, this is a good intention of the government, but doesn't it increase moral hazard in a sense? Why not use another method? That is to lift the restrictions on bank loans to our real estate companies. Now these banks still have restrictions, and they dare not lend. In other words, can the delivery of houses be transformed from an exogenous push by the government to an endogenous demand of each real estate company? If it becomes endogenous demand, they will be willing to do it themselves, and they will have the motivation to deliver the houses. Moreover, price reductions should be allowed. Real estate companies are currently punished for lowering prices, but price reductions are a good way to promote the market.

Yandong Zhang: But houses are still restricted from purchase.

Yang Yao: Houses are restricted from purchase, and house prices are not allowed to fall. This is a strange policy. Isn't it said that house prices are high? Why can't house prices fall? It's great for real estate companies to sell houses quickly. Common people will buy them when the price drops to a certain level. The impact of real estate on our consumption is too significant. After buying a house, you have to renovate it, and there are a lot of expenses. There is great potential in the real estate sector, and we should pay more attention to it.

Yandong Zhang: It's still too early in the process of urbanization. Mayor Huang had six major trends in real estate in 2019. Due to time constraints, let's have each person leave a sentence on the outlook for the Chinese economy, starting with Professor Tian.

Xuan Tian: Our domestic cyclical problems now need to be addressed through macroeconomic policies, and I agree with President Liu that structural problems need to be addressed through reform. The direction of reform is marketization, legalization, and internationalization, which is the direction of our country's institutional reform.

Yang Yao: In one sentence, I have confidence in the Chinese economy.

Yuanchun Liu: Global turmoil is precisely the opportunity for our economic rise.

Yandong Zhang: I agree with Professor Yao's view. Thank you very much. Due to time constraints, our China Economic Outlook this morning has come to an end. Let's give a round of applause to our guests. Thank you. The forum will continue in the afternoon.

CHAPTER 3

Global Financial Turbulence and China's Financial Market

Abstract Does the US banking risk lead to a financial crisis? Does the US banking turbulence impact China's economy? How did the Chinese respond to the international risk? This section discusses the above questions and gives the following viewpoints: First, although the US banking industry is in turmoil and the US regulatory authorities have taken swift measures, the risk of a crisis triggered by the turmoil in the banking industry has not been fundamentally eliminated. The impact of the US banking industry will not only spread within the banking system but also spill over into other areas. The risks of turbulence in the US banking industry have not completely passed. Second, from China's perspective, both government departments and domestic institutions should deeply examine the economy situation. We need to consider maintaining the security of external financing and the security of foreign assets. Also, we need to pay attention to the possible spillover effects of a dramatic shake-up in US stocks. Third, although the recent turmoil in the US banking sector spread the panic globally, it will not lead to a financial crisis in China.

Keywords US banking crisis · China's economy growth · Fiscal and monetary policy · Post-epidemic restart

J. Ju (ed.), *2023 Global Financial Turbulence and Economic Outlook*,
https://doi.org/10.1007/978-981-97-0206-0_3

3.1 Crisis, Not Turbulence

Tao Guan, Global Chief Economist at BOC International (China) CO., LTD.

Thank you, Chief Peng, I am very happy to participate in this discussion. I would like to talk about the impact of global financial turmoil on China's finances. First, I am a pessimist because, historically, since the 1980s, every time the Federal Reserve has raised interest rates, it has basically ended in a financial crisis. So, at the beginning of last year, I judged that there were four scenarios for the spillover effect of the Fed's tightening on China. Among them, the third scenario is that excessive tightening by the Fed may lead to the bursting of asset bubbles and trigger an economic recession. In March last year, on the eve of the Fed's interest rate hike, I said that the challenges faced by Powell would be greater than those faced by Volcker. At that time, Volcker had to choose between growth and price stability, while Powell had to face three difficult choices: stabilizing growth, stabilizing prices, and stabilizing finance. In October last year, I participated in an event and proposed to prepare for the next global financial crisis. At that time, I pointed out that the huge floating losses of bond investments caused by the soaring US Treasury yields might trigger financial risks. Although there were no signs of institutional failures at that time, unfortunately, my words came true. In early March this year, the Silicon Valley Bank incident was mainly triggered by the huge floating losses of bond investments, which led to panic selling and a run on the bank.

Second, although the US banking industry is in turmoil and the US regulatory authorities have taken swift measures, the risk of a crisis triggered by the turmoil in the banking industry has not been fundamentally eliminated. From March 10th to May 1st, three US banks have collapsed, with total assets of 548.6 billion US dollars, exceeding the total asset scale of US bank failures in 2008 and 2009 combined. I think it can no longer be simply called the turmoil in the banking industry, but rather a crisis in the banking industry. The key is that this wave of shocks has not completely passed, and after the problems of the First Republic Bank, some regional banks are still under tremendous pressure.

In addition, at the Fed's interest rate meeting in May, it has already hinted that it may raise interest rates for the last time, but it also emphasized that cutting interest rates is not the baseline scenario. In this case, the market is relatively optimistic, believing that the Fed may cut interest rates as early as September this year. In such a situation, either the Fed is wrong or if the Fed is wrong then the market also has a problem, as current risk assets have not fully valued the impact of the US economic recession. If the Fed is right and the market is wrong, the market needs to reprice the Fed's tightening. Therefore, from this perspective, the adjustment of US risk asset prices has not yet ended.

Third, the impact of the US banking industry will not only spread within the banking system but also spill over into other areas. Now, not only do small and medium-sized banks face the pressure of losing growth, but large banks also face problems with deposit liabilities due to the continuous high-interest rate environment, leading to a contraction in bank credit and increasing the pressure on economic adjustment. This is also an issue discussed by the Fed at two meetings. The Fed discussed whether to pause interest rate hikes, and one consideration was that the turmoil in the banking industry leading to credit contraction would affect the economy and prices, similar to the effect of raising interest rates. So far, the effect has not been revealed. We can see that with the Fed's continuous tightening and the continuation of the high-interest rate environment, the follow-up impact of interest rate hikes will further manifest. In this sense, the risk of the US banking industry's turmoil leading to a financial crisis and causing an economic downturn or even recession still exists.

In addition, the impact of the turmoil in the US banking industry on China has several aspects.

First, in terms of China, we need to consider maintaining the security of external financing. For example, after the issue with Silicon Valley Bank emerged, because it is a venture capital bank, many Chinese companies used this channel for overseas financing. People are worried that problems with these banks will affect the financing of venture capital companies overseas. This is financing security.

Second, the security of foreign assets. We saw that after the issue with Silicon Valley Bank, the stock market value of the US banking industry lost more than 54 billion US dollars, and this issue is still developing and evolving. Especially if many banks fail, their market value will basically be reduced to zero. If we step on a landmine, the loss would be quite significant. This includes the US banking crisis spreading to other areas, such as the commercial real estate sector. In previous years, a profitable investment was buying industry real estate REITs, with a return of 5%

or 6%. If commercial real estate prices adjust, these investments may face certain risks. This is the security of foreign assets.

Third, we need to pay attention to the possible spillover effects of a dramatic shake-up in US stocks. Historically, we have seen that basically every time US stocks fall, A-shares cannot remain unscathed. We don't know if this time will be different, but at least we should be vigilant in this regard.

Finally, regarding cross-border capital flows and the RMB exchange rate, there are both favorable and unfavorable factors. Overall, the impact of the Fed's tightening on China's external market is to some extent smaller than last year, and the RMB exchange rate trend this year depends more on the recovery of the Chinese economy.

In summary, the risks of turbulence in the US banking industry have not completely passed. From China's perspective, both government departments and domestic institutions should deeply examine the economy situation, find out the bottom line, make contingency plans, and that's all I have to say. Thank you.

3.2 The Impact of the Federal Reserve's Continued Interest Rate Hike and China's Response

Jianguang Shen, Chief Economist at JD.com

Peng Wensheng: Thank you, Chief Guan Tao. The main point is that the problem has not ended, the crisis has not ended, and it will continue to evolve, affecting the US economy and other countries.

Next, please welcome Chief Shen Jianguang.

Jianguang Shen: I am very happy to participate in the Tsinghua PBCSF Chief Economist Forum. I have been involved since the beginning, and I am very fortunate.

This morning, I listened to the talks about the US economy, including the US financial market. Dr. Guan Tao's speech just now is very consistent with what Mr. Roach and Professor Zhu said this morning. The financial turmoil in the United States will continue, and it will have a more profound impact on the global financial market or economy. I actually agree with this point very much.

In the past two years, I have done a series of research and articles on the US economy, mainly talking about US inflation. Two years ago, I said that US inflation is definitely not temporary, and it will last for a long time and have a profound impact. Here, I will show you a few pictures that vividly illustrate where the problem lies in the United States. The United States has experimented with Modern Monetary Theory this time.

As you can see from the top chart, the performance of the Federal Reserve and the European Central Bank's balance sheets. In 2008 and 2009, the Fed doubled its balance sheet, which is after quantitative easing. This time, the speed and scale of expanding the balance sheet and printing money exceeded that of 2007 and 2008. Now, with large-scale money printing, the money is given to the public through fiscal laws. This is the root cause of why this round of the United States has caused so many problems. In fact, it has a deep background and reasons, which is the practice of Modern Monetary Theory.

At the same time, we also see that the fiscal stimulus adopted by the United States in response to this epidemic shock is basically 5 times that of the 2008 financial crisis. As shown in the lower left chart, according to the International Monetary Fund's data, the United States has implemented a fiscal stimulus equivalent to 25% of its GDP to escape the impact of the epidemic. We know that the US fiscal deficit is also very high. What does it rely on? It relies on the central bank printing money to finance the fiscal spending. I think this is the most critical reason. The fatal flaw of the new monetary theory is inflation. This time, inflation in the United States has reached the same level as in the 1970s. Although the chart seems to show that it is lower than in the 1970s, the actual weight has changed. The Federal Reserve has conducted research, and according to the original weight, the current inflation is the highest in history. I remember that Governor Zhou Xiaochuan has always said that the US approach is like a pie falling from the sky. Printing money for the people seems to revive the economy, but in fact, there are sequelae, and the sequelae are inflation. What is the result of inflation? It is a sharp increase in interest rates. We see that the Federal Reserve has raised interest rates sharply, with the most and fastest rate hikes in history over the same period, resulting in a very obvious outcome. In the end, banks can't stand it anymore. Banks set prices based on the assumption that interest rates will not rise sharply. No one knows more about the US banking industry than the chairman of JPMorgan Chase. He said that the crisis will continue to erupt and is far from over. We see that on the one hand, banks continue to go bankrupt, and on the other hand, the US real estate market, the US real estate market transactions are now basically falling off a cliff. These two factors combined lead to overall financial turmoil, and it is far from over. We are only halfway through.

This time, because the scale of US rescue assets has exceeded that of 2008, the impact seems smaller than in 2008, because at that time, there was no rescue, and Lehman Brothers was allowed to collapse. This time, it was all supported by fiscal policy and other major banks. In the end, JPMorgan Chase took over with the backing of the US Treasury. This impact is not only in the United States but also has a significant international impact.

For example, in Sweden, unexpectedly, the president of the Swedish government's pension fund was removed. Sweden did not expect that every bank that went bankrupt would be affected. This impact is far-reaching. In addition, one of the largest real estate funds in the United States, Finland's real estate, has encountered problems. Many influences are intertwined, so the negative impact on our financial market, macroeconomy, and overseas this year and next year will continue. For China, I attended the International Monetary Fund's economic outlook for Asia in Hong Kong the day before yesterday. The director of the Asia Department also came to Hong Kong. The IMF predicts that Asia's contribution to global growth this year will reach 70–75%, mainly from China and India. Only these two major economies have had their growth forecasts raised, while growth in Europe and the United States has been downgraded. Of course, China's 4.5% growth in the first quarter is also better than market expectations, mainly due to the significant rebound in the tertiary industry, which is closely related to the recovery after the epidemic.

Of course, there are both good and bad data in the statistics. The good data is that we see GDP data and exports. In March, exports increased by 14.8%. Of course, there are some specific factors here because it does not quite match the export delivery value data announced by the customs. Many exports here rely on inventory backlog and order release. I think we should not take exports lightly. Therefore, I think the central government's current decisions, including the Politburo meeting and the State Council executive meeting, are very timely in stabilizing foreign trade and foreign investment. This morning, we discussed a lot about consumption. I think consumption is the key to China's economy this year. On the surface, retail sales rebounded sharply in the first quarter, but the main trends were in catering and travel, which showed obvious retaliatory rebounds. However, the main retail products, such as automobiles, communication equipment, household appliances, and retail in the first quarter, still showed negative growth. Therefore, durable consumer goods have not shown a significant recovery. Of course, there is the issue of unemployment. We see that the overall unemployment rate published by the National Bureau of Statistics is improving, but the unemployment rate for young people is increasing. Household savings have risen sharply, indicating that the willingness to save has increased significantly.

Infrastructure, this year, may have more room to stimulate consumption than investment because investment in infrastructure grew by 10.8% last year. Now the key is corporate investment. In the first quarter, one of the worst macroeconomic indicators was the negative 20% profit of industrial enterprises. It is hard to imagine that a company would expand reproduction and invest if its profits were not good. So this actually shows that investment is still relatively difficult.

Therefore, my policy suggestions, which were discussed this morning, include many measures to promote consumption, such as cash subsidies and consumption vouchers for low-income groups, home appliance subsidies for rural areas, and purchase vouchers. For companies that employ a large number of workers and actively comply with social security payments, further reductions in social security and housing provident fund rates can be made to encourage companies to increase employees. Especially in Hong Kong, it is clear that although it was said in the morning that there is no need for consumption vouchers after the epidemic, the real effect of stimulating consumption can only be seen after the epidemic. During the epidemic, issuing consumption vouchers had no effect. Therefore, the Hong Kong government has issued consumption vouchers for three consecutive years, and the effect is good. There are still ways to stimulate consumption, and the effect can be reflected. I will share this first, thank you.

3.3 Prepare for Global Downside Risks, Set Goals, and Establish Reasonable Economic Expectations

Ge Wu, Chief Economist at Changjiang Securities

The previous two speakers have already covered a lot, and the more we go on, the more pressure we feel, with the most pressure probably on

Director Zhang. I always feel that when we study overseas issues, for various reasons, it seems a bit like scratching an itch through our boots. Perhaps it's because of the way I personally obtain information, or maybe it's because we are in China. I often wonder how we can be smarter than overseas researchers and get ahead of Wall Street analysts.

After so many years of effort and exploration, I personally feel that the difficulty is quite significant. The information we get is often passive. No matter how bearish we are on the United States, is it really developing in our direction afterward? To be honest, if everything were out in the open, I might think it's not too bad. The key is the hidden things, or some new indicators, or financial stability here, and overseas stability there, what impact does it have on China? I will discuss two issues:

The first question is, even if the Federal Reserve does not raise interest rates today, even if the banking crisis in Europe and America stops here, and everything is OK, what does it mean for China? Does it mean that we are already facing a bright future with warm springs and blooming flowers? No, because we know that any policy or event has a cause and a consequence, and this consequence is the further cause of what happens later. Therefore, in our research, we emphasize not the interpretation after the fact, but more on the forward-looking judgment. From various forward-looking indicators, even if the Federal Reserve stops raising interest rates now, and the central banks in Europe and America stop raising interest rates, the impact on the global economic cycle will be at least half a year or even more than a year. We can also learn from textbooks that many policies have lagging benefits.

Regardless of the subsequent impact of the Fed's rate hike or the national credit contraction caused by the banking crisis, which also plays the role of the Fed's rate hike, it means that in the next half a year to a year, China can see the global economic outlook across the Pacific, and the downside risks may far outweigh the upside risks for half a year to a year. Therefore, I think this is something we must prepare for in advance.

The second question is not only about the immediate situation but also about poetry and the distant future. It's not about whether stocks are going up or down, or whether the economy is cold or hot, but about people's inner expectations. This issue is often mentioned by the central government, including the weakening of expectations. We often heard a story called "The Boy Who Cried Wolf" when we were young. Even when children grow up and tell the same story, if it cannot be fulfilled, they will have doubts. For a country's government and central bank, if your judgments are constantly proven wrong by the market, will people still believe you? We are all adults; do we still believe in this "The Boy Who Cried Wolf" fairy tale?

We can feel that in the past period, especially the Federal Reserve in the United States has encountered such a sharp challenge. In the past, as you know, the United States tried to explore forward guidance, which means that as a voting member of the Federal Reserve, I would publish my views on the future from time to time, forming a dot plot of the Fed's future interest rate hikes. However, whether it is forward guidance or the belief that inflation was temporary at the time, these things have been constantly falsified by reality. After multiple falsifications and multiple games, people no longer believe you. Losing trust is a terrible thing.

In our past research on central banks and monetary policy, we believe that the highest realm of monetary policy is not fighting and killing, going to the open market to adjust interest rates and credit, but rather, the highest realm of monetary policy is similar to what Sun Tzu's Art of War emphasizes: winning without fighting. It's like Zhuge Kongming standing on the city wall, and when you see him, you believe him because he hasn't made many mistakes before, so you naturally retreat. If he says inflation is temporary, we believe him, and as a result, people don't rush to buy food, and indeed, inflation turns out to be temporary. Therefore, the establishment of credibility is very important.

Dr. Guan and Dr. Shen both mentioned such a proposition, which is about the huge difference between market expectations and the Federal Reserve's expectations. For example, the current consensus expectation on Wall Street's Bloomberg is that the Fed will raise interest rates by 25 basis points, and perhaps in the next few months, the market will have more consistent expectations, and the Fed will cut interest rates three times in the second half of the year. However, Powell does not seem to think so, at least from his words, and the message he conveys is that interest rates probably won't be cut. We haven't seen such a big divergence between the market and the Fed in many years. What does this big divergence mean? Either the market follows the Fed, or the Fed eventually follows the market, which generally means turbulence. I am highly skeptical and uncertain about the future, and I think this is actually more deadly.

Although we are talking about the other side of the ocean, I suddenly thought of the so-called weakening of expectations in China, and I think this is also crucial for China's decision-makers. No matter how many difficulties are encountered in implementing something, I expect and believe that in the future, some of the goals set by China, including economic growth and high-quality growth, will indeed be achieved, and the weakening of people's expectations is based on trust in the government and officials. Thank you.

Peng Wensheng: Thank you, Dr. Wu Gou. The first three speakers had different perspectives, and it seems that their views on the United States are all about further deterioration or volatility. Especially what Wu Gou just said, can we see the United States clearly from the other side of the ocean? I sometimes think about this question too. Indeed, there is an old Chinese saying, "You can't see the true face of Mount Lu because you are in the mountain." Sometimes distance is beautiful, and you don't communicate with market investors every day. Short-term fluctuations and emotions may be clearer. I remember in the second half of 2020 and the first half of 2021, when I communicated with our American clients, few people in the market were worried about the US inflation problem. This issue is not particularly affected by short-term emotional fluctuations, and it may be clearer. So let's talk about how we see the situation in the United States. In fact, I believe that many online and offline audiences today are particularly interested in understanding how we see the United States because this is indeed a very critical factor affecting the global market. Next, please welcome Professor Zhang Xiaoyan.

3.4 Challenges and Reflections on the Banking Crisis in the United States

Xiaoyan Zhang, The Xinyuan Chair Professor of Finance and Associate Dean at PBC School of Finance, Tsinghua University

Xiaoyan Zhang: In order to participate in today's forum, I specifically went to the United States for a visit and just returned yesterday afternoon after a 30-hour flight. So if I say something wrong, it must be because I haven't adapted to the time difference yet. I literally went to the United States to see how the American people live in such a time.

What impressed me most was that I brought US dollars in cash, and the price of some items has increased significantly. For example, I ordered a latte every morning at the hotel, and it cost 7 dollars without tax or tip. When I was in the United States before, it was 3.5 dollars, so inflation is indeed quite severe. On the other hand, I saw a sad point. I went to Miami to attend an annual meeting of institutional investors, and I took a taxi from the airport to the hotel. The fare was still 37 dollars, which actually didn't increase, and I only gave an 8-dollar tip. So you can see that the price of a latte is the same as the tip I gave to the driver, so I think the American people are really living in difficult times. During the institutional investor conference, several articles discussed inflation. When institutional investors talked about the articles, they said that there was another interest rate hike. Obviously, there has been a lot of discussion on this topic in the United States in the past few years, and everyone is a bit tired of it. What I said is similar to the previous guests, but I also have some new and different aspects. So, this time I went to the United States to truly investigate a few thoughts on the American banking industry.

First, let me briefly talk about the Silicon Valley Bank incident that started in March this year. Look at the chart on the right, you can see its price dropped from over 200 to a few tens of dollars in one day, and three weeks later it was acquired by the First Citizens Bank of the United States. This is the first crisis. What you may not realize is that we have been talking about small and medium-sized banks in the United States. How small is Silicon Valley Bank? It ranks 16th in the United States. To give you a perspective, it is quite small. It encountered a run and was quickly stopped by the Federal Reserve and FDIC to prevent the rapid spread of the crisis. In fact, Silicon Valley Bank was saved. Then the run continued, and Signature Bank was closed. How small is Signature Bank? It ranks 29th among commercial banks in the United States. By April, the protagonist became the First Republic Bank, which ranked 14th. Now we have lost 14, 16, and 29, and they were acquired by JPMorgan Chase, right? JPMorgan Chase said that we responded to the government's call to acquire this bank. Everyone said that we can finally catch our breath. On the day I arrived in the United States, JPMorgan Chase took over the First Republic Bank.

But we still can't catch our breath, because the panic continues to spread to other banks. Here I have put two regional banks, one called Western Pacific United Bank, which plummeted by 50% on May 4th, and Western Alliance, which plummeted by 38%. So we have to talk about both sides of this issue. First, has it formed a huge crisis that swept all the big banks in front of it? It doesn't seem to have. The chart on the right shows the four major banks in the United States. They have fallen and been affected, but they have not fallen as badly as these small and medium-sized banks. The decline is more severe for the Western Alliance Bank and United Bank on the left. Now, the big banks are negatively affected, but not as heavily as the small banks, which are facing a fatal blow.

Everyone will ask why this is happening, what will happen next, and what impact it will have on China? It is because of the economic downturn, inflation, and the Federal Reserve's continuous interest rate hikes to cope with inflation. On May 3rd or 4th, during the recent FOMC meeting, the interest rate was raised for the tenth time, and it has now reached 5–5.25%. This is the highest level since 2007, and the increase is indeed quite significant.

In the process of this interest rate hike, do these companies also have their own responsibilities? Many media reports show that these banks themselves have some operational issues and gaps in risk control. One point I want to mention that people don't talk about much is that these banks have a high concentration of customers and businesses, especially Silicon Valley Bank. Why did it cause such a significant impact? Because it used to be a star bank with its own advantages. Silicon Valley Bank serves technology and innovation companies, Signature Bank focuses on digital currencies, and First Republic Bank targets high-net-worth clients. These banks have their own advantages, rising quickly when times are good and falling sharply when times are bad, exacerbating panic. During the bank run, the media and word of mouth spread the news that the bank was going to collapse, which played a significant role in spreading panic among the public. Social media also rapidly disseminated this panic.

On May 3rd, the latest interest rate hike took place. As several experts mentioned earlier, this might be the last interest rate hike, but it's hard to say. The Federal Reserve's statement downplayed the issue of tightening, suggesting that interest rate hikes might stop in the future. The announcement came out at around 2 o'clock, and the stock market fell in response. I cheekily checked the performance of the CSI 300 the next day, and it didn't seem to be too affected. So many online and offline friends and guests asked, what impact does this have on China? The impact of this interest rate hike on May 4th was not too bad. People are worried about whether the banking crisis will become a global crisis, but I don't think it has reached that point yet. The reaction in Europe is not significant, and the response from Chinese banks is not significant either. Will there be a possibility of further collapses among local small and medium-sized banks in the United States? I think there still is.

Lastly, I want to say, as Dr. Peng mentioned earlier, in the second half of our discussion, we will talk about how China is full of confidence. This is not what we are saying; it's what the IMF is saying. The IMF has lowered its global economic growth rate, with growth slowing in developed economies, but the main growth comes from emerging economies. How much does China contribute? 34.9%, making it the largest and most critical engine for global growth at the moment.

That's all I have to say. Thank you, everyone!

3.5 The Government's Support for Financial Institutions Continues to Strengthen

Wensheng Peng, Chief Economist at China International Capital Corporation (CICC)

Thank you, Professor Zhang Xiaoyan. I would also like to add some thoughts on the recent turmoil in the US banking sector. The previous experts have provided excellent explanations of the recent developments, causes, and future evolution of the situation. I will share some of my recent insights and thoughts. The CICC Research Department has also conducted a lot of research in this area recently, and there have been many internal discussions on how the recent banking events will evolve in the future.

I think there are two aspects worth considering beyond what the previous experts have mentioned:

The first is the role of social media in this crisis, as mentioned by Professor Xiaoyan earlier. I remember in 2008, many small banks in the United States went bankrupt, but there was no bank run on deposits at that time. The US deposit insurance mechanism still played its due role, and in hindsight, the FDI actually made money. This time, there was a run on deposits, which hasn't been seen for many years. Of course, there are other reasons, but one possible reason is the herding effect brought about by the promotion of social media.

I remember that in 2021, the capital market had already shown this. In 2021, retail investors were shorting the market, and social media played a very important role in this. Not only social media but also smartphones. When the financial crisis occurred in 2008, Apple's smartphones had just come out, and many online banks did not exist. Now, it is too easy to move deposits, taking only a few seconds or minutes, and there are many sources of information. In this sense, this crisis has brought a new challenge to future governments or global regulatory agencies. If you are interested in this, our research department's strategy group has a doctor who published an in-depth report a few days ago explaining this issue. In his report, he listed that if banks have not realized losses, floating losses, the floating losses of Silicon Valley banks are not the largest, and the floating losses of other banks are much larger than those of Silicon Valley banks. I suggest that you can find this report and take a look. This is my first impression, that is, the turbulence of the financial market in the new era may have some new characteristics in the digital economy and digital technology era.

The second point is related to this. How to deal with the herd effect and the spread of panic caused by social media? What should the government do? I don't know. What I can think of is a comprehensive guarantee, which means the government takes the bottom line. Because there is no way to stop the spread of panic on social media in the short term. What the Federal Reserve and the US Treasury have done this time, if you want me to understand, is a comprehensive guarantee. Although the tone of their statements at different times is different, sometimes they say it is not a comprehensive guarantee, but the actual objective effect, in my observation, is a comprehensive guarantee, not only for deposits insured by FDIC but also for uninsured deposits exceeding $250,000.

So, what is the difference between this financial crisis or banking crisis and the one in 2008? I feel that the first one is social media and digital technology. The second is the government's guarantee, which is more powerful than the last time. A while ago, either The Economist or the Financial Times published an article summarizing the evolution of government guarantees and support for the financial industry in Western countries, represented by the United States, since World War II. I think the rate of that evolution is very interesting, and this support is constantly strengthening. We generally understand that the government's guarantee was more powerful in the 1950s, 1960s, and 1970s when government control was stricter. In the 1980s, financial liberalization meant that the guarantee was not as strong, but in fact, the government's guarantee has been continuously strengthened over the past 70 years. This time is a typical example, and it is still worth our consideration, that is, what does the government's guarantee really mean?

As the expert mentioned earlier, we are now witnessing a strange phenomenon: when banks encounter problems, the interest rate rises to

5%, increasing from 0 to 5% in just over a year. The growth of the US M2 money supply has gone from over 20% in 2020 to a negative 4% now, which is a significant monetary contraction. However, the market performance remains quite good. If we look at the US stock market and the performance of US credit bonds, the market is very optimistic. How can we explain this? Of course, we can say that the time has not yet come, and the monetary contraction may take another half a year or a few months to fully manifest. There might be another explanation, which is the role of government support in reducing the market risk premium. In other words, government support actually boosts everyone's confidence. If this logic is correct, what does it imply? The original impact of monetary contraction on the economy and inflation control was through credit contraction, which occurs when the financial sector faces problems. The financial sector indeed has problems under tight monetary conditions, but policy support is limited, restricting the impact of bank problems on overall credit contraction.

What is the implication behind this? The overall financing conditions consist of the risk premium and the risk-free interest rate. The normal transmission mechanism is that the risk-free interest rate rises, and when it reaches a certain level, financial problems arise, leading to an increase in the risk premium. At that time, there is no need to raise interest rates further, as the increase in the risk premium will cool down the economy and bring down inflation.

Will this situation occur this time? Due to the US government's support, the risk premium may not rise as quickly or as high as before. If this is the case, what does it mean? It means that the risk-free interest rate needs to rise even higher, implying that the market's expectation of three rate cuts in the second half of the year may be too optimistic. The government's support makes the current expectation of rate cuts overly optimistic. What does this imply? I think this has significant implications for other countries and emerging markets. The reason for the rise in US interest rates, whether it is due to an increase in financing costs, risk premium, or risk-free interest rate, has different implications for other countries. If the US risk premium rises, the impact on other countries may not be as significant, as investors may be less optimistic about the United States, which is a relative performance. If the risk-free interest rate rises and the US Treasury bond yield increases significantly, the impact on other countries may be relatively more significant. Therefore, I think this is also worth our attention. How will this situation evolve? My personal view is that government support, especially from the US government, is not a good thing for overseas markets in the future, as the risk-free interest rate and the Federal Reserve's interest rate hikes will not decrease as quickly as the market expects. There may also be an important implication for the US domestic market: as the risk premium decreases and the risk-free interest rate continues to rise or remains high for a considerable period, it means that the financial risk pressure is shifting from the private sector to the government sector. With the risk-free interest rate remaining at a relatively high level for an extended period, what will happen to US government debt? In recent days, there has been much discussion about the debt ceiling, which is a significant issue, as the burden of interest payments is heavy. If the risk premium rises, leading to a decrease in the risk-free interest rate, the economy will still be affected by cooling measures, but the pressure on US government debt will be reduced. Now, with government support, the pressure of private sector debt defaults has decreased, but the pressure on government debt has increased. How will this situation evolve? Of course, many people say that it is unlikely that the US government will default, but with such high-interest payments, how can they be absorbed? So, I think these issues are worth considering: one is the impact of social media and the digital economy, and the other is the potential consequences of government support.

3.6 Discussion: Global Financial Turbulence and China's Financial Market

Wensheng Peng, Tao Guan, Ge Wu, Jianguang Shen, Xiaoyan Zhang

Wensheng Peng: That concludes our first round, where everyone shared their main views. Now, based on the different aspects discussed earlier, we can have some interaction, exchange, and discussion. First, let me ask Dr. Guan Tao, as an expert in exchange rates, how do you see the future trend of the US dollar and major currency exchange rates under such circumstances, and what does it mean for the RMB?

Tao Guan: First of all, I think everyone has discussed a lot, and talked more than I did, especially many interesting points were raised. I would like to make a few supplements.

Just now, Dr. Peng Wensheng mentioned an article that I have also studied. Under normal circumstances, the liquidity ratio is appropriate according to tradition. However, in an era of more developed media, the traditional approach to dealing with liquidity needs may not be sufficient in extreme situations. I have studied that piece of work.

Secondly, you mentioned the government's bottom-line support. As far as I can recall, after the 2008 crisis, major banks also faced a run, and Western banks either guaranteed all deposits or raised the limit. Measures were taken at that time, including in the United States and the United Kingdom.

Wensheng Peng: That was later.

Guan Tao: This time, the response was faster than that. Recently, China Finance published an article by the chairman of our Deposit Insurance Fund. He talked about the Silicon Valley Bank incident. On March 7th, Silicon Valley Bank was rated as the best bank in the United States for five consecutive years. However, on March 8th, a fire sale occurred, and the bank's stock price plummeted due to a run on March 9th. It was acquired on March 10th. Initially, the Federal Reserve and FDIC thought it was an isolated case, but after evaluation, they found systemic risks, so they issued a comprehensive guarantee on March 12th.

Wensheng Peng: Let me interrupt for a moment. In 2008, it was after the stock market crash and a significant widening of credit spreads.

Tao Guan: Yes, that was a post-event intervention, but the deposit insurance was eventually used. Just now, you mentioned an interesting point about the impact of government guarantees. In my opinion, it only suppresses the short-term risk of contagion, but the root cause is not resolved. With the United States still facing relatively high inflation, government guarantees, whether through fiscal support or central bank liquidity support, will ultimately affect the Fed's anti-inflation mission.

As you mentioned earlier, the Fed's tightening has a transmission mechanism that affects credit spreads and credit risks. The interrupted transmission leads to a slower response and a longer duration of high inflation. Regardless of whether interest rates will be raised, it means that the window for future rate cuts will be pushed further away. This will result in a heavier debt burden for both enterprises and governments. I think the biggest difference between Powell and Volcker is that Volcker had to choose between two options at that time, but now Powell has two burdens: high debt leverage and high asset prices. Regardless of whether there is an asset price bubble, asset prices are definitely high. Before the incident at Silicon Valley Bank on March 8th, the minutes of the Federal Reserve's Phase 1 meeting on February 1st were released at the end of February. At that time, the concern was not about financial stability risks, but about the risks of overvaluation in the US stock market and real estate. The situation had not yet been adjusted, and under such circumstances, it was a game of mutual offset between the left and right hands, which could make the Fed's anti-inflation task more complicated. Therefore, it is not to say that it can be used arbitrarily. Interestingly, the Federal Deposit Insurance Corporation (FDIC) recently released a draft soliciting opinions on deposit insurance system reform proposals, proposing three options: first, raising the deposit insurance limit; second, full insurance; and third, providing insurance for some corporate deposits, possibly not at $250,000, but raising it to a certain limit. However, each option has its pros and cons, as insurance coverage comes at a cost and can also cause market distortions. I think this is quite interesting.

Returning to your question about the impact of the Fed's tightening on the US dollar exchange rate, the current mainstream market view, or at least the impression the Fed gives to the market, is that the Fed's interest rate hikes are nearing an end. Regardless of whether there will be a rate cut at the end of the year, the possibility of high-interest rates and restrictive monetary policy continuing for some time remains. Under such a backdrop, the support for the US dollar this year from interest rate differentials, which drove its appreciation last year, will weaken. However, I feel that this year, whether in the United States or Europe, there will be many stories to come in this aggressive tightening environment. I think the US dollar's trend this year may be more driven by risk aversion, with more chaos in the global economy and international finance providing support for the US dollar. Moreover, from a historical perspective, after the collapse of the Bretton Woods system, we can see that the US dollar does not necessarily bottom out immediately after each Fed rate hike cycle ends, and it may still maintain a period of strength.

One reason people are bearish on the US dollar now is the Fed's easing, but in fact, not only is the Fed easing, but the European Central Bank and the Bank of Japan have also implemented negative interest rates. They also have unlimited easing. Europe has already exited negative interest rates, but Japan is still implementing them. From a fundamental perspective, the US economy is better than Europe and Japan. Therefore, from a fundamental perspective, according to the US dollar index, it cannot fall and will not fall. Under such circumstances, I think if there is no major crisis this year, the US dollar may maintain a relatively strong trend, without significant appreciation. If there is a significant appreciation or turbulence, there may be a wave of decline after a medium–high trend. As for the RMB, as I mentioned earlier, the impact of the Fed's tightening on the RMB was relatively significant last year, but this year, the main factor affecting the RMB exchange rate is not the external environment, but the recovery of the Chinese economy. The high probability event this year is that the world economy is going down, while the Chinese economy is going up. However, the rebound of the Chinese economy is a high probability event, but how high and how good the quality is, is the real key to determining the strength of the RMB. Policies from the Fed and fluctuations in the US dollar exchange rate may have some short-term disturbance effects on the RMB, but if we look at a slightly longer period, say one year, the key variable determining the RMB's trend this year should be the post-epidemic restart of the Chinese economy.

Wensheng Peng: The post-epidemic restart still depends on the height of economic recovery. Following this, let me ask Dr. Shen Jianguang, your PPT also mentioned that the recovery of China's economy this year is very important for consumption. Your company, JD.com, also has some high-frequency data in this area, which can help us track and analyze the evolution of our consumption more quickly and timely. Can you share some of your recent analysis and research in this area, including the May Day holiday, these high-frequency data, the May Day holiday is the service industry, but are there any noteworthy aspects in the commodity sector?

Jianguang Shen: Some data is not convenient because the annual report has not been released yet, but I think, in fact, the overall consumption pattern in March's macro retail data is still very fully reflected. My PPT shows that the National Bureau of Statistics' retail data in March shows that large items, such as automobiles, household appliances, and home renovations, are still experiencing negative growth in the first quarter. This can be seen, and I think the Politburo meeting also said that the recovery momentum still needs to be improved and is insufficient. It is obvious that travel, catering, service-oriented, and contact-based consumption have rebounded significantly. The first quarter data from the National Bureau of Statistics is also very clear, but the real core retail indicators have not yet seen a recovery. This macro data is actually similar to the micro data. What is the reason for this? The first is income. Economists make consumption models based on income. The growth rate of income is not as fast as before. The growth rate seems to be a little higher than the fourth quarter of last year, but it is still relatively slow. Secondly, we saw that the newly added resident deposits in the first quarter of this year reached 9.9 trillion yuan, a record high, and everyone's willingness to save is very strong.

Wensheng Peng: How to explain this?

Jianguang Shen: The following data will illustrate this. The first is the employment situation. Now the employment of young people, in January and February, the national statistics data for 16–24-year-olds is 18.1%, and in March it is 19.6%, a jump in just one month. As mentioned this morning, it is not yet June or July. If it reaches June and July, many college graduates will be included in the statistics. Under such circumstances, what else is added? In the first quarter, we also saw that the profits of industrial enterprises above the designated size announced by the National Bureau of Statistics were negative 20%. This background is not stable for employment and income expectations. Last year's economic work conference and this year's Politburo meeting also mentioned the need to increase residents' disposable income, which is very important. Therefore, I see that the country has recently taken measures, including a large number of recruitments in government agencies, enterprises, and public institutions, and the country has also provided 1 million internship positions. These are targeted measures. As discussed this morning, to trigger consumption in the short term, I think what is lacking now is the post-epidemic measures to push demand back to normal. For example, consumption vouchers and cash vouchers are still very necessary. It is not that one-time consumption vouchers and cash subsidies can bring the economy to a sustainable track, but they can push it to a normal track. With additional measures, it can lay the foundation for this year's recovery. This is my point of view. Consumption vouchers have been discussed a lot, but the general feeling is that consumption vouchers are one-time. However, as you know, after Hong Kong issued consumption vouchers, small and micro enterprises, shops, and restaurants have demand, and they have income. In fact, it also helps them survive on the supply side. In addition, the tax reduction and fee reduction policies that our government used to like can be combined to exert force on both demand and supply simultaneously. This year, I am still looking forward to a policy like ours that can push the economy toward recovery. Moreover, I would like to add that Dr. Peng just mentioned a very interesting topic, which is the regulatory policy in the United States, and the regulation is completely different. I just want to briefly mention that it is very interesting. Recently, the president of JPMorgan Chase in the United States has also begun to reflect. He believes that many bank problems are actually regulatory problems, and the entire regulatory framework in the United States has problems. Government bonds are risk-free, and it is found that Silicon Valley Bank now holds bonds, nothing else, not many assets, mostly holding the government, so-called risk-free, but the risk is huge, which is a great lesson.

To go deeper, recently, the US National Security Advisor Sullivan has reflected on the US industrial policy and the New Washington Consensus. I think this represents a new direction, that is, the United States now includes financial policies, regulatory policies, and macroeconomic policies. In fact, there is a point that the traditional concepts of the past are still problematic. I think this is getting closer to China, especially the emphasis on industrial policies, especially on regulation and government guarantees. China's regulatory agencies provide guarantees, so everyone is not panicking, and there has never been a panic. They are now learning, and I think this can be studied in depth. China's regulations are also evolving, but in fact, the United States is now increasingly reflecting on its problems and learning from our regulatory framework, not only in terms of industrial policies but also in financial policies and financial regulation. I will just add this here.

Wensheng Peng: Dr. Jianguang just spoke very well. Regarding consumption, we need to look at the economy from multiple perspectives and some comprehensive indicators, not just GDP and some bright things. I have also been thinking about this issue, including looking at GDP itself. In fact, the consumption indicators themselves are not weak, and there are some bright indicators, but why does everyone feel that it is not so good? We can say that unemployment is still relatively high, some young people are unemployed, and how do we look at economic indicators? My biggest feeling is that the prices are too weak, and of course, the demand behind them is weak, which is the biggest problem. Although our GDP is not bad in terms of actual GDP, CPI is only about one, and PPI is negative. The overall PPP parity index is very weak, indicating that the pricing power of enterprises is relatively weak. Therefore, under such circumstances, we know that in the early stage of the economic recovery cycle, enterprises do not have much confidence, and everyone is still observing each other, whether the business is really improving, and whether it can be sustained. Everyone is still hesitant.

What about the next step? Observing well, it is indeed sustainable. The first is to raise prices, then expand production and employment. Therefore, in this sense, we are still in the early stage of recovery. This is not surprising because we are only 3 or 4 months away from the relaxation of the epidemic in December. So in this sense, we may still be in the early stage of recovery, but because of the particularly low base in the fourth quarter of last year, some numbers look beautiful now, so everyone has high expectations. In fact, we are still in the early stages of recovery.

The regulation mentioned by Jianguang just now is also a very interesting issue. Regulation actually has regulatory costs. I tend to agree with the saying that our Chinese banks are state-owned banks, while American banks are not state-owned banks but public–private partnership banks. Why are they public–private partnerships? Because regulatory agencies represent the government's deep involvement in the commercial operations of banks, so there are regulatory costs. The more complex and detailed the regulation, the more likely it is to affect efficiency. Of course, this is in line with our current global direction, from efficiency to safety, from efficiency to stability.

Following this logic, I would like to ask Chief Wu, Dr. Wu has long-term work experience in the central bank and has two or three books in this area, which are excellent academic works. Recently, many people have raised questions about the practices of the Federal Reserve, and some say that the Fed is learning from the Chinese central bank because, on the one hand, it is tightening quantitative easing and reducing its balance sheet, and on the other hand, it is rescuing troubled banks and providing liquidity loans. Liquidity loans are actually targeted, and you can understand them as structural monetary policy tools. The Chinese central bank has been implementing structural monetary policy tools, which are not in line with the past 40 years of neoclassical mainstream economics and macro policy framework, with interest rates as the guide, and central bank interest rate regulation is enough, and other things should not be managed. How do you view this issue, and can you make some comments?

Ge Wu: I understand this issue in this way. We have all studied physics, and when physics studies problems, it often studies the situation without friction, where there is no friction force, and the object maintains a uniform speed or some other speed when pushed by hand. However, the real economy has friction or some serious structural problems. So, you will feel that the same amount of money is put down, although the total amount is put down, but you will find that the money is not discerning, such as in China, as we all know, we have budget hard constraint departments and budget soft constraint departments. Therefore, money will be retained in some special state-owned enterprises and private enterprises due to guarantees and other reasons. Including recently, we have seen that the financing costs of many state-owned enterprises are relatively very very cheap, and this is still the case.

So, monetary policy is generally about the total amount, but I personally think that in economies with some structural problems, it should also take into account some structural issues. However, my personal bottom line is that the overall policy cannot be deconstructed because, as a government and as a central bank, how can it be smarter than the market and know that the money will definitely go where you want it to go? Including the recent early repayment of loans, many people have borrowed money in the name of loans for small and medium-sized enterprises through business loans and consumer loans to buy houses. At that time, our business loans and consumer loans were targeted to support small and medium-sized enterprises. You find that the money goes to where it thinks it is most needed, even though the regulatory authorities do not allow this practice, but there is still early repayment due to structural distortions or policy distortions.

Everyone present, or friends online, have you repaid your loans early, and why did you repay them early? Is this a problem caused by the overall issue or is there a structural distortion inside?

So, to simply answer Bloomberg's question, we have many structural policies, and fiscal policy has more structural functions. Monetary policy can do some structure, but I personally don't think it should do large-scale structure. We think there should be perseverance in this regard because, from my understanding, whether the policy is strong or weak, perhaps the United States is going to another extreme, but where China is going also depends on the degree of control. This is the first point.

Secondly, regarding the short-term issue, why are people confused? It's because we feel that we have experienced a once-in-a-century pandemic, and our current recovery is the recovery after a pandemic that has not been seen in a century. So how can we naively know what the public is worried about, what entrepreneurs are worried about, and what the government is pondering? There is no precedent for this. The three-year pandemic, in the past years of reform and opening up, if we regard the pandemic as a supply shock, we have not experienced such a long supply shock. Therefore, under such circumstances, I am increasingly skeptical about some of our inherent judgments, including our current pandemic recovery, and the debate on Bloomberg about whether it is in the middle, early, or late stage, which is highly debated in the market. In terms of month-on-month growth rate, the fastest month-on-month growth rate has passed, but the year-on-year growth rate has not come yet. Last year's second quarter Shanghai pandemic, the year-on-year growth rate in the second quarter was very eye-catching, but in terms of our perception of the month-on-month growth rate, many companies and residents may feel that the month-on-month growth rate has come down a bit, but some month-on-month growth rates have not yet started, such as international travel has not yet started, a large number of industries, including real estate, catering, and various data, the fastest month-on-month growth rate has passed.

At the same time, we are welcoming, just now discussing the external, discussing the external of course is to build a human destiny community, we have the world's mind, but more importantly, what impact will it have on China? If everyone's discussion just now is correct, even if the Federal Reserve is calm, the lag will also affect our external demand, and the challenges in the second half of the year are not small in my personal understanding.

Therefore, under such circumstances, I think there is another important issue that is invisible and intangible, that is, when we talk about a so-called, you can call it damage to the balance sheet, or you can call it a scarring effect, how strong is this effect? Now we can feel it, including the issuance of consumption vouchers mentioned by Dr. Shen, no problem issuing consumption vouchers, Beijing has been discussing this topic for more than a year, but who will issue them? From our observation of the balance sheet, especially the local balance sheet, they were affected earlier, the corporate balance sheet was affected, the household debt was affected, where does the money come from, and where do we create employment opportunities? This is a question worth our real consideration, but overall, what I expect is that the data may be deceptive, not that the data is deceptive, but that our observation of the data is biased.

I have a deep impression that in 2021, everyone remembers that it was the second year after the Wuhan pandemic. At that time, it was also seen that due to the low base in 2020, the economy was doing well in the first half of 2021. Therefore, in the second half of 2021, or in the middle of the year, many policies were adopted, which I personally understand as contractionary policies. So later, as everyone knows, the central government immediately realized, including the central economic work conference mentioning the three major pressure issues several times, these issues are related to our judgment of the data and the real judgment of the economy.

Now, our whole country, especially the central government, is calling for a great research atmosphere. How to scientifically and comprehensively view the data is important. How is the year-on-year comparison, and how is the month-on-month comparison important? Thank you.

Wensheng Peng: I think one of the very important points that Wu Ge mentioned is that we need to look at the data comprehensively. In fact, when we do economic analysis and some technical analysis, sometimes the quarter-on-quarter and year-on-year comparisons are indeed very controversial. Each country is different; the US GDP is quarter-on-quarter annualized, of course through seasonal adjustments, while China and most countries prefer to look at year-on-year comparisons. Who is right? I think each has its own merits. If you can really make good seasonal adjustments, such as the Chinese New Year factor and the US Christmas, quarter-on-quarter may be a better reflection of the latest changes. However, this important premise is under normal circumstances. Under abnormal circumstances, such as the impact of the pandemic, quarter-on-quarter is meaningless because you encounter sudden statistics, and the quarter-on-quarter decline in one quarter may be very severe, and the next quarter may rise very sharply. Just like the first quarter of this year, the quarter-on-quarter growth was strong, 2%, 2.1%, annualized 8%, but is it really that strong? It's because the fourth quarter of last year was weak, so at this time, it's more meaningful to look at the year-on-year comparison, because many economic indicators do not occur simultaneously. For example, the employment price just mentioned is the cumulative effect of economic activities, so in this sense, looking at the year-on-year comparison also has its rationality. So we need to look at it comprehensively. Combine quarter-on-quarter and year-on-year with other indicators, such as employment and prices.

Ge Wu: I would like to add that what Dr. Peng Wensheng said is correct. I just want to remind everyone that this year's economic data and the vast majority of economic data are based on a very low base last year. If you look at the 10-year government bond yield, when the 10-year government bond yield encounters such base disturbances, the smart market 10-year government bond yield is not rising with the public opinion speed, but with the quarter-on-quarter economic growth rate, including the quarter-on-quarter growth after seasonal adjustments. You can see the financial market, the first quarter data is very good, but because your quarter-on-quarter growth rate has already come down, or the quarter-on-quarter expectations have already come down, the 10-year government bond yield is going down. As a view of so many participants on the future economic outlook, it is reflected in the price. Therefore, for decision-makers, of course, as Dr. Peng Wensheng said, both are needed, but this year is after all a period of post-pandemic recovery. And from the experience of various countries, why is it said that it is a once-in-a-century pandemic? The word "century" is very important, or the "century pandemic recovery" is very important? We need to be fully prepared mentally. Although we have not experienced it, objectively speaking, some countries are ahead of us in epidemic prevention and optimization, especially Asian countries. Objectively speaking, their year-on-year growth rate and quarter-on-quarter recovery are the fastest in about one quarter. After one quarter, when the spontaneous recovery is eliminated, more needs to rely on endogenous economic momentum recovery or some policy protection, external support, and the economy can stabilize relatively. So I think on this point, our Central Economic Work Conference is still sober, there is recovery, but it is not endogenous, spontaneous, my subtext, this kind of policy protection is important, vigorously investigating and researching, knowing the most intuitive feelings of the people, I think it is important.

Wensheng Peng: What you said should be known to the market, so everyone realizes that the quarter-on-quarter growth in the first quarter is abnormal, and it will come down later, so the interest rate does not reflect the strength of the first quarter. This also proves that we cannot just look at the quarter-on-quarter growth, but need to look at it comprehensively.

Jianguang Shen: It is obvious that we must not look at the year-on-year comparison in the second quarter, and we must look at the quarter-on-quarter comparison in the second quarter, considering that the second quarter of last year was a low base.

Wensheng Peng: So, we cannot just focus on the month-on-month or year-on-year comparisons. We need to consider the different impacts and influences brought by different time points. The last question, Professor Xiaoyan, you are in the education industry. What do you think about the impact of the pandemic on human capital over the past three years, online education, and the employment issues of young people mentioned earlier? This is not only a problem in China but also a global issue. What can we do to make up for the impact of the pandemic on human capital and future economic growth? I don't know if you have any observations and thoughts on this?

Xiaoyan Zhang: Dr. Peng suddenly put me in the position of an education expert, but my original profession is not in education. However, I am still very happy to share with you what we have seen during the three years of the pandemic.

I have recently been working on an interesting topic called Generation Z, which is about young people during the pandemic. We just talked about many social media topics. Nowadays, young people in their 20s and 30s have spent a lot of their youth online, making rational and irrational choices, earning and losing money. This may not be directly related to employment, but for me, an important topic is financial health. Financial health means having money, liquidity, and making rational plans for your retirement and lifelong wealth. In the past three years, I think many people here and online have already tried various capital markets through their smartphones and various apps, and they have probably learned about the relationship between risk and return. In this process, many people have been "harvested" as leeks, accumulated wealth management experience, been misled by social media, and learned how to calculate (English).

I think that during these three years of the pandemic, we have seen the next generation of investors, Generation Z. What I am most concerned about now is that, as Dr. Peng and other guests just mentioned, during the pandemic recovery stage and economic downturn, we are worried about high unemployment rates and a turbulent economic environment. I want to use the last minute to tell everyone that, as an educator, we still need to learn some basic financial knowledge, understand the fundamentals of the market, and not be swayed by online bubbles like the GameStop incident in 2021. If everyone knows the fundamentals, they won't be swayed, even though some short sellers were squeezed out, and the stock price of GameStop eventually returned to its fundamentals. Recently, the bank run on Silicon Valley Bank and other major banks has been mentioned, with many social media factors involved. The GameStop incident was about the stock price going up, while the Silicon Valley Bank incident was about the stock price going down. People rushed to withdraw their money due to undervaluation, causing unnecessary risks. My suggestion is not macroscopic. I hope that all students and friends, both online and offline, can pay more attention to basic financial knowledge, focus on some fundamentals, improve their financial literacy, and become knowledgeable individual investors.

This is my biggest wish as an educator.

Wensheng Peng: Thank you, Professor Xiaoyan Zhang. We have already exceeded our time by 1 minute, but this session was still very good. We discussed the economic and financial markets, the current situation, the problems we face, and some future highlights and risks. I personally feel that our discussion was quite enlightening, and I hope our audience and listeners feel the same. Thank you to our four guests and to all the listeners for participating.

CHAPTER 4

Global Financial Turbulence and China's Economic Outlook

Abstract The theme of Roundtable III is **Global Financial Turbulence and China's Economic Outlook**. In this part, we have invited **Haizhou Huang,** Managing Director and Chairman of Capital Market Committee at China International Capital Corporation; **Xunlei Li**, Chief Economist at Zhongtai Securities; **Haibin Zhu**, Chief China Economist at J.P. Morgan; **Ting Lu**, Chief China Economist at Nomura; **Bin Zhang**, Senior Fellow, Deputy Director of Institute of World Economics and Politics, Chinese Academy of Social Sciences, to discuss about the economic phenomena and development issues in their respective fields. Firstly, Haizhou Huang gave an introduction to the background of the international financial market. He has stressed that developed countries had outperformed emerging markets in terms of this year's performance, with Europe being relatively brilliant. Secondly, Xunlei Li recognized that the current pressure on local government debt in China is still relatively large, then he offered five suggestions. Thirdly, Haibin Zhu talked about his judgment on China's macro economy and then focused on the issues of Chinese real estate market. Fourthly, Ting Lu compared the current situation with the past few economic recovery periods in our country to deepen our understanding of the current economic situation. Fifthly, Bin Zhang shared his advice about how to use price measures to expand demand. Then, the economists of this theme held a discussion with two important questions: (1) what is the biggest risk for the world or China

J. Ju (ed.), *2023 Global Financial Turbulence and Economic Outlook*,
https://doi.org/10.1007/978-981-97-0206-0_4

in the coming quarters? and (2) what is the most urgent need for China to do? especially the policy suggestions.

Keywords Geopolitics · Economic policy · Globalization · Real estate industry

4.1 Global Financial Situation and Market Opportunities

Haizhou Huang, Managing Director and Chairman of Capital Market Committee at China International Capital Corporation

I am very grateful to the host, Bin Zhan, and to Tsinghua PBCSF Chief Economist Forum for inviting me to participate in today's meeting. I will first give an introduction to the background of the international financial market as requested by the host, so as to facilitate the following speakers to build upon it and engage in targeted discussions and exchanges.

I have prepared a PPT and will briefly go through it with everyone. This is about global financial trends and market opportunities. In fact, I heard a little bit about this in the previous session, but not much. Since 2023, the global market has seen a rise in risk appetite, so in this sense, the overall performance of the equity market has been relatively good, including A-shares, H-shares, US stocks, and other stock markets, with Europe actually performing quite brilliantly. If we look at the performance, 2023 might be an interesting phenomenon compared to 2022. The performance in 2022 might be the worst, such as Bitcoin, the five biggest technology companies, NASA, etc., while this year's performance is relatively good.

In 2022, of course, the important theme for developed countries was anti-inflation. Some anti-inflation themes performed slightly better, but in fact, the market volatility of anti-inflation themes in 2023 was quite large, which can be described as a triple kill in stocks, bonds, and foreign exchange. The foreign exchange here refers to the US dollar exchange rate, and other countries' currencies have experienced significant declines against the US dollar.

In terms of this year's performance, overall, developed countries have outperformed emerging markets, with Europe being relatively brilliant. If we look ahead to this year's situation, I think there are two key variables: US inflation and China's growth. US inflation mainly refers to the rapid decline in US inflation and when the Federal Reserve will stop raising interest rates. If the Federal Reserve cannot raise interest rates, I think this is an important aspect. As for China's growth, this year has been a relatively good year for China's overall growth. The market also expects the growth to be above 5%, including experts, investment banks, and CICC, which all put growth at 5.5%, while the IMF's expectation is 5.2%. Global growth has encountered significant difficulties this year, and a growth rate of 5.2% or 5.5% contributes about one-third to global GDP growth, which is a significant contribution. Of course, looking back, to clarify this issue, we need to discuss the early high inflation, which mainly occurred in the United States and Europe, and this is a significant problem. The main reason for this in the United States and Europe is obviously related to the extremely loose monetary policy and fiscal stimulus adopted by developed countries, which occurred after the COVID-19 pandemic in 2020. As you can see from the overall chart, after the COVID-19 pandemic in the United States, the growth rate of M2 actually exceeded 20% and even reached 25%. The speed of the Federal Reserve's balance sheet expansion was also very fast. In fact, after April 2020, the Federal Reserve expanded its balance sheet by 3 trillion US dollars in 6 months. After the 2008 financial crisis, the Federal Reserve conducted three rounds of quantitative easing from 2009, with a total expansion of about 3 trillion US dollars, which took 5–6 years. This time, it was 6 months, and the scale was very different. Due to fiscal policy, as you know, when the United States started the TEP, the fiscal stimulus actually increased the deficit by 300 billion to 500 billion US dollars. From April 2020 to April 2021, the US fiscal deficit reached an astonishing 6 trillion US dollars, accounting for about 30% of GDP. I think the reasons behind this are directly related to the three rounds of quantitative easing and QE4 I just mentioned. The scale of QE4 is more than the total of the three rounds.

However, we need to think about why the Federal Reserve and the US Treasury Department adopted such large stimulus measures. I think an important reason is the concern about uncertainty at the time. The market was mainly worried that the United States would experience a major financial crisis like in 2008 and 2009, and some people believed that the United States would experience a Great Depression like in 1929–1933. Therefore, based on these concerns, the stimulus measures were excessive in hindsight. However, under the circumstances at the time, they felt they should spare no effort, similar to the European debt crisis in 2012, which is very clear.

There is another background. After 2008, the economies of developed countries around the world entered a relatively low-growth state. Especially after 2012, the economy of the European Union and the Eurozone, experienced zero interest rates, negative interest rates, and low growth. This is actually related to the low growth after the financial crisis in Japan in 1990. The Japanese experienced they lost 10 years, then found out they had lost 20 years, and then lost 30 years. In fact, these 30 years can be simply summarized as three zeros: zero interest rates, zero growth, and zero inflation. The 30 years of zero growth had a significant impact on the Japanese economy. In 2012, you may remember that former US Treasury Secretary—*Lawrence Summers* gave a famous speech at the IMF, arguing that developed countries, including the United States, mainly referring to the United States, would experience long-term growth stagnation. This is because if the economy falls into a long-term deflationary state, that is, low-interest rates and low inflation, it will be accompanied by very low growth. Therefore, in this sense, US policymakers were actually worried that the United States would suffer from capital disease. So, it was not only due to concerns about the Great Depression but also concerns about this disease that the measures taken were excessive.

If we talk about what the Federal Reserve has done right, I think the policies adopted by the Federal Reserve and the US Treasury have been quite effective in protecting the balance sheets of households and businesses. As we can see, after the outbreak of COVID-19 in 2020, the "three balance sheets" of the United States, which are actually the financial institutions, businesses, and household debt ratios, have risen sharply, as can be seen from the left chart that it is soaring upwards. In fact, these three lines were pressed down directly because the United States made a swap. That is, the US fiscal deficit was raised by 30 points, and direct transfer payments were made, which can be seen clearly from the right chart, the government sector and private savings lines are basically a negative correlation, which is actually achieved through transfer payments.

In hindsight, what did the Federal Reserve do wrong? It is obvious that the magnitude was too large, the speed was too fast, and the expectations were also wrong. But what I want to say is that this expectation has a concern about the possibility of a major depression in the United States in the future, and at the same time, it wants to avoid the United States falling into a Japanese-style lost 10 years, 20 years, and 30 years.

If we talk about the more important reasons for inflation, there is another supply-side shock, the impact of the COVID-19 pandemic is actually longer than the market expectations and policy decision-makers' expectations, and of course, there is also the direct impact of European natural gas and oil prices brought about by the war. So last year, from the perspective of the capital market, anti-inflation themes such as oil and natural gas were relatively good topics.

The Federal Reserve began to raise interest rates significantly last year and raised them again in May, which may be the last time. The tight money in the United States has already become a de facto tight credit. Under the premise of tight credit, the growth rate of the US economy is slowing down, and to some extent, the US economy is heading toward recession. Of course, I will talk about it later, if it is a recession, it may be a relatively mild recession, and it can even be said that the United States may achieve a so-called soft landing.

The result is a slowdown in economic growth on the one hand. On the other hand, it has also triggered some problems in the banking system, which have recently attracted more market attention, from Silicon Valley Bank to First Republic Bank. Growth is also weakening, but from the public data, some indicators, such as employment and consumption, are relatively stable. It is not ruled out that the United States may have a soft landing. That is, the Federal Reserve will stop raising interest rates from now on and may not cut interest rates before the end of the year allowing the economy to continue to slow down, and let CPI inflation move toward 3.0 without rushing to bring CPI inflation down to 2.0 so quickly. One reason is whether the leverage ratios of Chinese financial institutions, businesses, and residents are sufficient. We just discussed the leverage ratio, which soared directly in 2020, and this process of soaring leverage ratio was suppressed by the US fiscal swap.

The current tight credit and weak demand have clearly begun to ease the pressure on core inflation, and we may expect overall inflation to be around 3% by the end of this year. Therefore, interest rates continue to fall, and may return to 3% by the end of the year, which is for several years of government bonds. In terms of interest rate hikes, the May hike may be the last one.

The situation in Europe is better now than it was at the end of last year, because at the end of last year, due to oil, natural gas, and other factors, as well as concerns about winter, it was thought that the problems might be more significant. Europe experienced a warm winter, so natural gas prices have seen a noticeable decline, and inflation in Europe has eased. However, the inflationary pressure faced by the Eurozone, including the UK, is greater than that of the United States, and the Eurozone and the UK have not yet encountered significant banking problems, including the core countries of the Eurozone and the UK. In this sense, the impact of interest rate hikes has yet to be reflected.

If we look at the changes in market expectations from the end of last year to now, the market's expectations for the growth of the US economy are marginally worse, while the expectations for the European economy are moving in a better direction. In other words, the market initially thought that Europe would experience a deep recession. However, Europe may also be able to avoid a deep recession, so in this sense, the marginally better situation is being repaired in many places.

The US economy was initially thought by many in the market to be able to avoid a recession with a baseline of a soft landing. Now, this is still the baseline, but I believe that the probability of a soft landing in the United States is still quite high.

Japan experienced a significant depreciation of its currency last year. The Bank of Japan chose to continue lowering interest rates between maintaining exchange rates and interest rates, resulting in significant currency depreciation. In order to prevent the market from forming a consensus expectation, certain operations were carried out. In April, the Bank of Japan appointed a new governor. In this sense, there are still some market expectations for the new governor's measures, but there has yet to be much change so far. Therefore, although Japan did not have an income inflation problem before, the adjustment of interest rates in Japan means that the World Bank governor's speech is still relatively positive, and the so-called normalization of monetary policy continues to be delayed. I am looking forward to discussions later.

The rise in US interest rates and European interest rates, as well as the tightening of liquidity, are significant backgrounds for banking crises. It is worth noting that it does not mean European and American banks will experience a systemic crisis, including US banks, and deposits have not left the banking system. From small banks to large banks, small banks have a more direct impact on regional development, so it will be more difficult for small and medium-sized enterprises to obtain loans, which will lead to a slowdown in the growth of the US economy and regional economies. However, the risk of causing a systemic banking crisis is relatively small.

There is little room for progress in tackling banking crises, and the Federal Reserve's response to relevant policies is still relatively timely. As I just mentioned, the overall leverage ratio of the banking industry is low, and the balance sheets of households and businesses are good. This year's IMF Annual Meeting Economic Outlook has been slightly adjusted downwards, but not much, basically raising China's economic growth slightly. The IMF's full-year forecast for the United States is 1.4, which cannot be said to be a recession or a significant recession, although the GDP growth in the fourth quarter may be close to 0 or near 0. China's growth is 5.2, the Eurozone is 0.7, some Eurozone countries may be close to 0, Germany is 0.1, and the UK is -0.6, with the UK facing more significant risks. My judgment is here, and I will now hand it over to the host.

4.2 Five Measures to Reduce Local Debt Risk

Xunlei Li, Chief Economist at Zhongtai Securities

Thank you, Bin Zhang, for hosting. I will also share my PPT, and my presentation will mainly focus on the issue of local government debt.

The current pressure on local government debt in China is still relatively large, especially as many institutional investors, including banks, are worried about whether local government debt will be delayed or defaulted. Indeed, our economic growth rate is declining, especially after three years of the pandemic, and this issue has become more prominent.

Let me briefly review and then offer five suggestions.

First, since 2015, local government debt in China has continued to expand, with the main increase coming from special-purpose local government bonds. By the end of 2022, the total general debt balance was 14.39 trillion yuan, with special-purpose bonds exceeding 20 trillion yuan, totaling about 35 trillion yuan. Since 2019, the year-on-year growth rate has been above 15%, nearly three times our actual GDP growth rate. This means that the growth of debt is much faster than the growth of the economy, indicating that the efficiency of our economic growth still needs to be further improved. This does not even include the astonishing growth of local financing platform debt.

The excessive growth of debt will lead to a possible decline in future fiscal expenditures. For example, this year's nominal fiscal deficit rate is 3%, which may be lower than last year. Our fiscal policy also proposes to improve quality and increase efforts to raise the quality. The reduction of urban investment bond issuance during the past three years of the pandemic has significantly impacted local finances. However, the pressure will be more significant in the future. PPP investment in new projects has been declining since 2018, dragging down infrastructure. The downturn in the real estate market will also significantly impact local government land finance. Therefore, the current pressure on local government finances is arguably the largest in history. There is no exact data on the scale of urban investment bonds. We have also compiled statistics here. Since 2011, the interest-bearing debt of urban investment in China has expanded rapidly, with an annual guarantee of more than 10%. By the end of 2022, the total interest-bearing debt of urban investment in China reached nearly 52 trillion yuan, an increase of 6.7 times compared to 6.8 trillion yuan in 2011. Many provinces and cities have seen land transfer fees covering less than 100% of government debt interest, such as Liaoning, Guizhou, Guangxi, Chongqing, Inner Mongolia, Xinjiang, Qinghai, Tianjin, Gansu, Jilin, Yunnan, Heilongjiang, and Tibet. Affected by market squeezes, financing costs in some weak areas have risen rapidly. The investment return rate of urban investment platforms, as predicted by our ROIC, has dropped from 3.1 in 2011 to 1.3 in 2022. This is also worth paying attention to. On the one hand, we need to invest heavily to maintain stable growth. On the other hand, the return on investment is declining, which means that the greater the pressure to maintain stable growth, the greater the debt growth. Therefore, it is difficult for the local government's debt balance to see a decline in growth rate.

Some localities have taken extreme measures to try to marketize local debt, especially platform debt, by letting the market bear the risk. This practice shows that defaulting cannot reduce financing costs. For example, Henan Yongmei's default harmed the credit bond market in Henan Province and even the whole country. Therefore, defaulting cannot solve the debt problem and will worsen the regional credit, leading to significant financing difficulties and higher financing costs for local governments and state-owned enterprises. Therefore, from a development perspective, it is necessary to maintain government credit and not default easily. So, these problems objectively exist, and I have five suggestions:

First, reducing the cost of debt. There is still much to be done, such as local governments issuing debt through policy banks or commercial banks' low-interest funds to reduce the cost of debt. I believe that if there is such a policy as support and guarantee, local commercial policy banks or commercial banks are also willing to use relatively low-interest funds to reduce the cost of local government debt.

Second, extending the debt term. Non-bond debt can be postponed, such as the Zunyi Road and Bridge loan extension.

Third, revitalizing state-owned equity. Local governments had confidence in expanding debt in the past because they had land finance as support, especially in economically developed areas. Their land finance revenue was considerable and could cover the interest on the debt. Land finance has gradually diminished, with the national land transfer income decreasing by nearly two trillion yuan last year. In this context, I suggest increasing the reform of state-owned enterprises, following the requirements of making state-owned enterprises stronger, larger, and better, so that the valuation level of state-owned equity can be raised. There are many ways to improve the valuation level, such as using equity as collateral for banks, which can also obtain low-cost financing, and obtaining fiscal revenue through equity transfer. By improving the quality and efficiency of state-owned enterprises, their operating income can be increased, and through equity transfer, mergers and acquisitions, and reorganization, fiscal revenue can be obtained on the one hand, and the valuation level can be improved on the other hand, thus further reflecting the financial strength of local governments.

Fourth, expanding the existing space of local governments. Although local debt has become a prominent and necessary issue, whether local debt can maintain credit stability is also a topic of great concern to us. In terms of the total amount of local debt, it is not enormous compared to China's economic strength. Moreover, although our country faces the pressure of aging before getting rich, compared with Western economies, their debt ratios are relatively high, but they have entered developed economies. Their pressure may come only from the pressure of population aging. However, we are not only facing the pressure of population aging, but our economy is still in the middle and high-income stage, not a high-income economy. In the future, under the pressure of an economic downturn, we still need to maintain economic growth, which will inevitably lead to debt growth, so the future growth space of our debt should be relatively large. The sum of the central government's and local governments' debt balances, plus the hidden debt balances of various localities, is roughly equal to 100%. However, compared to the US federal government's debt of more than 130% and Japan's government debt accounting for about 250% of GDP, our debt balance as a percentage of GDP, that is, the government's leverage level, is not considered high. Moreover, China's government is a country with public ownership as the main body, and our government has many assets. The total assets of state-owned enterprises alone exceed 300 trillion yuan, plus land, forests, water resources, and minerals, most of which are state-owned. Therefore, if the total assets of the Chinese government are used as the denominator, our leverage is even lower. In the same caliber as Western countries, our overall debt has a lot of room for expansion. The space for local special bonds in 2022 is only 1.1 trillion yuan, and the space for general bonds is only 1.4 trillion yuan. I think we can still expand.

Fifth, further optimizing our current investment projects, using special-purpose bonds for investment and project arrangements. As I mentioned earlier, our local platform debt's overall return rate is relatively low. In the future, we should limit the use of special-purpose bonds, especially in the field of transportation infrastructure. Currently, our total mileage of highways ranks first in the world, but the average number of vehicles per kilometer is very low. Our highways are already excessive compared to other countries, which leads to a low ROIC return rate. Against the backdrop of an accelerating aging population, we still need to ensure that our investments are used in areas related to people's livelihood, such as pensions, healthcare, and expanding consumption. We should increase investment in these areas appropriately. Because our economy needs to transform, we need to shift from the past investment-driven model to a consumption-led model or invest in new infrastructure-related areas with higher investment returns, such as new energy, new materials, 5G, artificial intelligence, etc. We need to increase investment in infrastructure in these areas. The debt pressure is mainly due to concerns about the large space for future debt expansion. Reducing debt costs, extending debt terms, optimizing debt structure, etc., and exchanging time for space, if done well, our current expectations for future development will be further enhanced. From the capital market perspective, if our expectations rise, risk appetite can also be improved, and the material level can be raised, which is beneficial to achieving stable growth of the entire economy. These are some of my humble opinions. Welcome to criticize and correct them. Thank you.

4.3 The Real Estate Market Has Stabilized at a Low Level, With Obvious Market Differentiation and a Structural Downward Trend

Haibin Zhu, Chief China Economist at J.P. Morgan

Thank you, Bin Zhang. First, I will talk about my judgment on China's macroeconomy. The last table in Dr. Haizhou's presentation is the IMF's judgment on global economic growth. In the overall decline in global economic growth this year, China is a crucial counterbalance, and China's contribution to global growth may reach 1/3 or 40%. The year-on-year growth rate of 4.5% in the first quarter exceeded market expectations. For the year, achieving a growth rate of more than 5% is a consensus among various parties. We may be more optimistic, predicting that the year-on-year growth rate in the second quarter will return to more than 8% and the annual growth rate will be more than 6%. This is related to China's policy adjustments since the end of last year, especially the restart after the epidemic and policy corrections in some key areas (such as real estate policy/platform economy policy), which have led to economic recovery and rebound.

First of all, we need to pay attention to the fact that China and the world, especially the European, American, and Japanese economies, are asynchronous this year in terms of economic growth, inflation, or policy choices.

The second point is that, from the current perspective of China's macroeconomy, this round of recovery is not quite the same as before, and it is more driven by the restoration of consumption, led by the recovery of consumption and services from a low-level last year. At present, we do not need to worry too much about short-term economic performance. We need to focus on the sustainability of the economic recovery, for example, weak private investment and structural unemployment issues (the unemployment problem of young college students is still very serious). The two main areas that exceeded expectations in the first quarter were exports and the stabilization of the real estate industry at the bottom. Whether these can continue in the next few quarters needs attention. In addition, the front-loading of macro policies in the first quarter was very prominent, whether in fiscal or monetary policies, such as the record high of new social financing in the first quarter. Whether these policy support measures can be sustained will significantly impact our judgment of the sustainability of future recovery.

I just listed many questions earlier, and due to time constraints, I will now focus on one issue, discussing the Chinese real estate market. As mentioned earlier, in the context of the overall macro data exceeding expectations in the first quarter of this year, the real estate industry as a whole was the first to enter a bottoming out and stabilizing phase in some significant indicators, which should be considered a vital part of the many positive aspects of the first quarter's macro data. In terms of policy, the 16 real estate measures were introduced in November last year, and the financing conditions for real estate developers have improved significantly. After December last year, China quickly adjusted its epidemic prevention policies and entered a post-epidemic restart mode around the Spring Festival this year. Looking at the leading indicators of the real estate market, housing prices began to rise month-on-month in February and March, and new home sales also began to rebound significantly from the bottom. The decline in real estate investment slowed down from a 10% drop last year, a double-digit drop of 16% in the fourth quarter of last year, and a decline of about 6% in the first quarter of this year, significantly reducing the drag on the economy. Therefore, these are some encouraging signals we have seen in the real estate market in recent months.

At the same time, we need to see that the differentiation in the real estate market is still pronounced. The first is the differentiation between real estate market data. We just mentioned that new home sales and housing prices have shown signs of stabilization, but the other two indicators, new housing starts and land transfers are still very sluggish. In the first quarter of this year, compared with the same period last year, new home sales were flat, but new housing starts fell by 18%, and land transfer fees fell by 27% year-on-year in the first quarter compared to the same period last year. Therefore, this specific differentiation in the main indicators is a very important issue for the future trend of the real estate market. Of course, from an optimistic perspective, this could be a matter of the order in which various main indicators improve during the cyclical improvement of the real estate market itself. Generally, sales data will improve first, followed by land transfers and new housing starts. However, another possibility is that the decline in land transfer fees and new housing starts may be more structural. This is the first differentiation I want to talk about, the differentiation between the main market data.

The second differentiation is between different cities and sub-markets in the real estate market, which is also reflected in the current city-specific policy implementation for real estate.

The third differentiation is between real estate companies, especially state-owned enterprises, and private developers. From the data of February and March this year, new home sales generally improved, but mainly reflected in the sales of state-owned enterprise developers, which increased by 70% year-on-year, while among private developers, sales of risky developers fell by about 40% year-on-year in February and March, and sales of relatively stable private developers were only flat year-on-year. The data differentiation between state-owned and private developers is very serious.

These differentiations may significantly impact the basic judgment of the future real estate market. From this year's perspective, we believe there is a high probability that the real estate market indicators will stabilize at a low level in 2022 after a significant decline. Last year, new home sales in the real estate market fell by nearly 30%, and new housing starts fell by 40%. On this basis, this year will be a low-level stabilization, but the possibility of a rebound is still very small, and the entire market may be more about finding a new balance point at a low level. This is our baseline scenario.

From a causal perspective, although there was a significant adjustment in real estate policy after November last year, it is difficult for us to repeat the large-scale real estate stimulus policies of 2015–2016 under the premise that "housing is for living, not for speculation." For example, most cities have canceled purchase restrictions, and the central bank has provided monetized subsidies for shantytown renovation through PSL-targeted structural policies, directly creating new demand in the commercial housing market. In hindsight, the PSL stimulus in 2015–2016 led to the preemption of future real estate demand and affected the underlying factors of the real estate market. From a policy perspective, it is difficult to repeat the large-scale monetary policy stimulus of 2015–2016.

In addition, we have always emphasized that the decline in the real estate market in the past one or two years is not only a cyclical downturn after policy tightening but also reflects that the real estate market entered a structural downturn channel around 2017. In terms of the overall demand for commercial housing, it peaked in 2017 and then entered a structural downward channel. The decline in the main indicators of the real estate market in the past two years is more likely to return to the equilibrium level. Therefore, it is difficult for us to expect a significant reversal in the real estate market as in the past while the structural downward trend continues.

From a macro perspective, the drag on the economy from real estate this year will be less than last year because the drag was significant last year. Will the impact of real estate on the economy turn from negative to positive in the next one or two years? I think the possibility is low, and it is even possible that the negative impact of the decline in real estate investment on the economy will start to widen again in the next two years. Corresponding to the very important phenomenon mentioned earlier, we see the differentiation among the main indicators of the real estate market recently. Although sales and housing prices have begun to stabilize, new construction and land sales are sluggish, especially private developers are currently more focused on seizing short-term market opportunities, delivering buildings, and completely exiting the real estate market after completing existing projects. Suppose we rely solely on state-owned developers in the future, whose market share was only 30% before the pandemic. In that case, it is a big question mark whether they can maintain the relatively stable development of the real estate market in the future.

We just mentioned that the land transfer fee in the first quarter fell by 27% year-on-year. Last year's first quarter, compared to 2021, had already fallen by 27%, so our current first quarter land transfer fee has basically returned to the level of around 2017. This raises two issues:

First, real estate investment will decline in the next few years. Real estate investment basically corresponds to the cumulative number of land transfers and new housing starts in the past few years. If last year's decline, the land transfer fell by more than 20%, and this year is another double-digit decline, the real estate investment in the next few years is likely to be negative growth, and this negative impact on the economy may continue.

Second, returning to the point that Xunlei Li just mentioned about the pressure of the local government and local platform financing, this pressure may become a focus of our work. I may be more cautious about this point than Li Xunlei. First of all, in terms of the current debt level, there is actually little room for further expansion of debt. Although our public data shows that the central government's debt accounts for about 20% of GDP, the local government's special and general debt add up to about 30%. As Xunlei Li just mentioned, our local government financing platforms have more than 50 trillion yuan debts, accounting for about 45% of GDP. So if we add up the three items, it's 95%. In addition, a considerable part of corporate debt is state-owned enterprise debt. If we change the concept to public debt, our public debt may be second only to Japan in the world. Therefore, there may not be as much room for leverage as Li Xunlei just mentioned.

In terms of the future disposal of local government debt, according to this year's government work report, "preventing and defusing local government debt risks, optimizing debt maturity structure, reducing interest rate burden, curbing increments, and resolving stock," is in line with many of Xunlei Li's five suggestions. I am worried that it may be misinterpreted in practice as mainly through extension and interest rate reduction, but this often leads to a phenomenon of corporate zombification that occurred in Japan. After the collapse of the real estate bubble in Japan, there was corporate zombification and bank zombification. We are unlikely to adopt a market default mechanism for local government debt. However, if we do not take some swift, decisive, and diversified disposal actions, thesituation will likely be a long-term, continuous replacement of local government debt. If the problem of low investment efficiency is not fundamentally resolved, local government debt may eventually become a significant obstacle to the normal development of China's economy.

That's all for my speech, thank you.

4.4 The Economic Recovery Environment Is Complex, and Confidence Needs to be Boosted Through Structural Reforms

Ting Lu, Chief China Economist at Nomura

The previous speakers have elaborated on their views on the current economy from different perspectives. After learning from them, I have been greatly inspired and benefited. There is no doubt that our economy is currently in the post-epidemic recovery, but what are the characteristics of the recovery? How sustainable is it? Should macro policies continue to exert force, or should they be appropriately contracted? Where exactly is the bottleneck if the recovery cannot be sustained well? These are the questions we need to think about at present. To learn from the past and know the new, based on the speeches of the previous speakers, we can compare this with the past few economic recovery periods in our country to deepen our understanding of the current economic situation.

There have been two significant economic recoveries in the past ten years, one after the 2008 Lehman crisis and the other after the 2015 stock market crash. Compared with those two recoveries, this recovery has three significant differences.

First of all, the external environment is different, as Dr. Haizhou has just explained very clearly. The previous two times our country's economy recovered; it was tied to the global economic rebound. The recovery times and the magnitudes were different, but overall, the world was in a synchronized economic recovery. In contrast, this time, the starting point of each country's economic recovery mainly depends on the time when the pandemic ends. Most countries have significantly relaxed their epidemic prevention measures outside of China between spring 2021 and spring 2022, production and life quickly returned to regular, economic growth rates rebounded sharply, and inflation was triggered. Developed economies such as the United States and Europe experienced the highest inflation since the early 1980s, eventually forcing the United States and European central banks to raise interest rates significantly and rapidly from spring 2022. Affected by interest rate hikes and other factors, the economic growth rates of the United States and Europe began to decline significantly in the second half of 2022. For example, the US GDP growth rate fell from 3.2% in the third quarter of last year to 2.6% in the fourth quarter and 1.1% in the first quarter of this year, and it is very likely to drop below 1% in the second quarter of this year. Under the rapid interest rate hikes by the Federal Reserve, some medium-sized banks in the United States have recently experienced failures, which will inevitably have some negative impact on the US real economy. Therefore, despite some recent good indicators, the possibility of the US falling into recession in the year's second half is high. China ended its dynamic zeroing policy in early December last year, Herd immunity was initially formed at the end of January this year, and the economic growth rate began to rebound. Therefore, when our country's economy began to recover, the global economy, especially the economic growth rates of developed economies such as the United States and Europe, was in a rapid downward channel, which would constrain our country's external demand and exports. It is worth noting that China's export growth rate was 30% in 2021, 7% last year, and 0.5% in the first quarter of this year, with a very obvious slowdown. The 14.8% export growth rate in March was affected by some short-term factors and is not sustainable. The weakness of external demand will inevitably constrain the strength of our country's economic recovery this year.

The different external environment is also reflected in another dimension, which is geopolitics. We must objectively see that compared with the previous two recoveries, we are facing an extremely complex and difficult international environment in this recovery. China-US relationship is one of the most critical aspects of our country's foreign relations. After the China-US trade conflict outbreak in 2018, China-US relations took a sharp turn for the worse, and the pandemic and the Russo-Ukrainian war further deteriorated China-US relations. In recent months, we have been delighted to see our country's breakthrough in diplomacy, but the overall situation is still very severe. The impact of geopolitical issues on our country's current economic recovery is reflected in the following aspects. First, countries such as the United States have intensified their technology embargoes on our country, directly affecting our country's technological progress and industrial upgrading, as well as foreign direct investment and domestic manufacturing investment; Second, from the perspective of the global supply chain, the United States encourages multinational companies to transfer production capacity to the United States and its friendly countries through legislation such as the "*CHIPS Act*," which will also affect new investment in our country; Third, the impact on the confidence of our country's entrepreneurs and high-net-worth individuals, indirectly leading them to marginally reduce investment and consumption demand in the country; some people have a higher willingness to increase asset allocation overseas, which will also pose certain obstacles to our country's economic recovery.

The second significant difference between this round of recovery and previous economic recoveries is in the real estate sector, which Dr. Haibin has just elaborated on very profoundly. The real estate sector is extremely important, contributing about a quarter to GDP, and its impact on economic fluctuations may far exceed a quarter. This is because the real estate industry also plays a crucial role in transmitting loose monetary policy through the credit market. In the previous rounds of recovery, it is no exaggeration to say that real estate was the engine and leader of each recovery. In the last recovery in 2016–17, due to the considerable boost of the monetized shantytown renovation to the real estate market, the new loans flowing into the real estate industry once exceeded 50% of the total new loans of banks in the second half of 2016; while in the first quarter of this year, this ratio was only 6%. The real estate market experienced a brief post-epidemic rebound in February and March this year, but the rebound quickly weakened in April. According to the sales data of the top 100 Chinese developers, the sales area of new homes in April this year was only 53% of that in 2019, while the ratio was 65% in March. According to the National Bureau of Statistics, developers' newly started construction area in the first quarter of this year fell by 19% year-on-year, based on a 39% decline last year. We must not take it lightly for the real estate sector because of the recovery in some cities in the first two or three months.

The downturn in the real estate industry will also produce a series of spillover effects, especially in local fiscal matters, which Xunlei Li has also discussed very profoundly. Before the decline in real estate, the industry's contribution to local government finances exceeded 40%. However, in the first quarter of this year, local government land sales revenue fell by 27% year-on-year. Since it had already fallen by 23% last year, the national government land sales revenue has been halved. In fact, the situation is even worse because many places sold land to local urban investment companies. The difficulties in local finance will cause a series of chain reactions, ultimately leading to depressed total demand and reducing the sustainability of economic recovery. Moreover, since land sales are now mainly concentrated in first- and second-tier cities, the situation in most lower-tier cities is even more challenging. Because the real estate recovery varies greatly between regions and cities of different sizes, this round of recovery has solid regional characteristics compared to previous recoveries, and the gap between regions and between large and small cities has widened further. This widening regional gap, in turn, will suppress total demand, especially the actual investment demand of local governments. Since the beginning of this year, without the central bank cutting interest rates, although the economic growth rate has rebounded significantly, China's market interest rates have not only not risen but have also declined. The ten-year government bond yield has dropped from 2.92% at the end of January to 2.73% yesterday, indicating that China's real credit demand and investment demand are relatively weak.

The third difference between this round of recovery and previous economic recoveries lies in consumer spending. On the positive side, the consumption demand and supply previously suppressed by the pandemic will be released simultaneously, and the lifting of restrictions after the pandemic will have a significant pulse effect on the economy. The crowded major tourist attractions during the recent Golden Week manifested this effect, which was not present in previous recovery rounds. However, we should not be overly intoxicated by this retaliatory consumption rebound. This pulse effect is difficult to sustain because the pandemic and other factors have profoundly impacted residents' consumption capacity and willingness in the past few years. First, the scarring effect brought by the pandemic; Chinese residents have experienced three years of the pandemic, and apart from a few quarters, the lockdown has had a significant impact on service industries such as tourism, transportation, and catering, with many households experiencing sharp declines in income and substantial consumption of savings. Second, the negative wealth effect brought about by the contraction of the real estate industry, coupled with the sharp decline in land fiscal revenue, the salaries and other incomes of people within the system have generally declined to vary degrees across the country. Third, in addition to the impact of the pandemic and the downturn in the real estate industry, sectors such as education and training and platform economy have also undergone significant adjustments. These factors combined have led to a relatively high unemployment rate, especially a youth unemployment rate as high as 19.6%, and the number of "flexible employment personnel" has reached 200 million. Fourth, for various reasons, residents' expectations for future income growth may be lower than before the pandemic, increasing the intensity of precautionary savings. In fact, in the first quarter, China's smartphone shipments and passenger car sales fell by −13.8% and −7.3% year-on-year, respectively. It can be argued that these effects are already reflected to some extent.

We can make some judgments from the comparative analysis of these recovery cycles. First, we should not be overly optimistic about the better-than-expected GDP growth in the first quarter. We need to see that due to the pulse effect in service consumption, China's economy is currently in a sweet spot of post-pandemic recovery, but this sweet spot may be short-lived. In the second half of this year, the pressure and resistance faced by China's economic recovery are immense due to the factors mentioned earlier. Second, in terms of short-term macro policies, although we may not need to increase the intensity of easing and stimulus, it is not yet the time to exit easing policies, and we still need to carefully protect the current recovery achievements. Third, the bottleneck of the current economic recovery lies not in whether monetary and fiscal policies are sufficiently relaxed but in whether a series of structural policies can boost people's confidence again, stimulate people's enthusiasm, and allow the market to play a more critical role in the allocation of factors such as land and capital. At the first meeting of the 20th Central Finance and Economics Committee held yesterday, the central leadership made excellent arrangements. I think there are two points worth paying special attention to: first, to "adhere to openness and cooperation, and not to close the door and build cars"; second, to "cherish and protect outstanding entrepreneurs even more." If these two points can be well implemented, I believe the current economic recovery momentum can be sustained.

4.5 Achieve Rapid Economic Growth by Reducing Policy Interest Rates

Bin Zhang, Senior Fellow, Deputy Director of the Institute of World Economics and Politics at the Chinese Academy of Social Sciences

Next, I would like to briefly share with you a view on policy, and the topic I would like to share is using price measures to expand demand.

Now the situation seems relatively clear. On the one hand, our economy is recovering, but the price level is very low, with both CPI and core CPI at only 0.7%. This indicates that goods are not easy to sell, difficult to sell, and prices are not dared to be raised, which is one aspect. At the same time, the job market is still under pressure, especially for youth employment, and even the overall unemployment rate is relatively high. Moreover, we see the growth of wages, especially for the middle and low-income groups, and the growth of migrant workers' wages is only 1.5%, at the end of the first quarter, compared to the previous 7–8% growth rate, it is now only 1.5%. We can also see that the current economic growth rate is very low. After looking at individual numbers and putting all the numbers together, what does it tell us? It tells us a very clear message, which is a very typical situation of insufficient demand. By overlooking all the data, the main problem is not on the supply side, not efficiency, but insufficient demand, with low prices and low output.

Insufficient demand is reflected in two aspects. On the one hand, consumption is insufficient. Why is consumption growing and recovering, but the recovery speed could be faster and stronger? Our urban residents' income growth is only 4%, while before the pandemic, it was 6%, 7%, or even higher. We know that consumption depends on income growth on the one hand, and on the other hand, it depends on whether you are willing to spend the money given the income. In the past, urban residents earned 100 yuan and spent 62 yuan. During the pandemic, we earned 100 yuan and spent 57 yuan. Now that the pandemic has passed, how much do we spend when we earn 100 yuan? Has it all recovered? No, we still spend 57 yuan. In the first quarter of this year, we earned 100 yuan and spent 57 yuan, and there was no significant recovery. Indeed, our offline service consumption has increased, but our consumption of durable goods has actually declined. Together, the consumption tendency has not rebounded as quickly as imagined, which is the consumption aspect.

On the other hand, investment is also insufficient, especially in the private sector, with only 0.6%. Private investment is still lying on the ground. Private investment is the most important engine for creating employment and wage growth. With private investment at this level, it is difficult for our economy to achieve future employment, income recovery, and sustainability. Faced with this situation, how can you expand consumption and investment? We can also change this question. Expanding consumption under given income conditions means reducing savings. We can transform this question: how can you reduce savings and expand investment? In a market economy environment facing such problems, the first thing to use should be price means to solve the problem.

What price means? Textbooks tell us very clearly, and other countries also do the same, that is to use interest rate means, policy interest rates. Adjusting policy interest rates to drive various loan interest rates and bond interest rates to drop is what we should learn from the most, which makes savings income lower and investment income higher, and then reduces savings and increases investment. From another perspective, the so-called lowering of policy interest rates and various loan interest rates is actually a disguised way of distributing money, and the magnitude is even larger, at the level of several trillion yuan.

Why do I say that? Everyone can imagine that if our policy interest rate could have a very significant decline, and we, like some countries, lower the policy interest rate to zero when facing economic difficulties, the loan interest rate would be much lower than it is now. If the cost of repaying our debts, both principal and interest, is reduced by half or even more, higher interest rates mean higher asset valuations, housing prices will no longer fall, stock values will increase, and the monthly repayment interest will be reduced by half or more, making the balance sheet stronger. This would be the most tangible support for both consumption and investment.

We have also done some calculations ourselves, not very precise, considering only one channel. If the policy interest rate drops by 100BP, it could increase the cash flow of enterprises, residents, and the government by more than one trillion, and the nominal GDP growth rate would be 1.2%. From the experience of other countries, whether the United States or Europe, they have achieved their employment goals and economic growth rates close to potential growth rates by lowering interest rates. Japan used low interest rates for a relatively long time, emerged from the so-called lost 20 years, and the core of Abenomics is interest rate policy, which has helped them out of the lost 20 years. Adjusting through policy interest rates and price measures is also very effective.

There are many different opinions on interest rates and loose monetary policy this year, and I would like to talk a little more about it. For example, in the first quarter of this year, our M2 growth rate was 12.7%, which is very high, the highest in the past 5 years, and the peak of the past 5 years. People might say that since the money supply has increased so much and the economy has not improved much, is monetary policy useless? I think we need to clarify two points. First, we did not issue more money in the first quarter. On the one hand, we indeed saw an M2 growth rate of 12.7%, which seems like a lot of loans, but at the same time, we should also see that our social financing growth rate was 9.9%, which is the lowest point in the past 5 years. In the past, M2 and social financing were relatively consistent. Why is there such a big difference, one being the lowest point in the past five years and the other being the highest point in the past five years? An important reason is that many banks have been under pressure to lend in the past period, and who did they lend to? Many loans were given to platform companies, which did not borrow money in the bond market and did not carry out new financing in the bond market, but turned to bank loans, which had relatively low interest rates and better conditions. What is the result of such a conversion? This kind of conversion will increase your loans and deposits, but at the same time, new bonds will decrease. When combined, the total new financing of the whole society is not very high. Therefore, everyone should have a clear understanding of this data. In the first quarter, we did not issue more money, and social financing is a more comprehensive perspective for everyone to see how much money we have lent out, which is a relatively low point in the past 5 years.

Secondly, after we release the money, it does not form a well demand expansion. In a standard and reasonable situation, by lowering the interest rate, the interest rate cost is reduced, and the debt cost is reduced. At this time, whether it is consumer credit or willingness to invest because the interest rate is lower and the borrowing cost is lower, people will borrow money, spend money after borrowing, and form the next round of input, which will lead to a continuous improvement in demand. However, we did not do it this way. That is, we did not do it through interest rate means. How did we do it? We selectively told some enterprises that they could have a lower interest rate, only if I do think their industry needs to develop, I will give them a lower interest rate and lend them money, and for industries that are not particularly favored, my interest rate remains the same. What will this result in? We value those industries valued by banks or regulatory authorities and are willing to give them lower interest rates. However, will they spend the money from the perspective of counter-cyclical regulation after giving them money? We value many industries, especially manufacturing, and the investment in manufacturing is not based on the short-term amount of money, but on medium and long-term considerations. Many companies have received a lot of money and very low-interest rates while they do not really need the money. Many companies save the money after receiving it, have an interest rate difference, and do not spend it. If the money is not spent after borrowing, it is impossible to form demand, it is impossible to form the growth of the next round of income, and it is impossible to expand the market truly.

On the contrary, if many companies are not valued in this process, which we may name structural monetary policy, they will still have high interest rates. Although they want to spend money, invest, and consume, they are still blocked by high interest rates. Therefore, our way of easing monetary policy may also make the money sent out unable to create enough demand expansion. We also need to make some adjustments and reflections on this regard.

4.6 Discussion: Global Financial Turmoil and China's Economic Outlook

Bin Zhang, Haizhou Huang, Xunlei Li, Haibin Zhu, Ting Lu

Bin Zhang: Let's move on to the discussion session. The topics discussed in this session are critical and quite scattered because of various perspectives. I wonder if we can focus a little more during the discussion session and focus on discussing two questions. First, in your opinion, what is the biggest risk for the world or China in the next few quarters? Second, what is the most urgent thing that China needs to do? Especially now, there are various policy suggestions. In your opinion, what does China need to focus on the most?

Haizhou Huang: To start the discussion, the market is still somewhat worried about the European and American economies after the interest rate hike from a global perspective. I believe that the core issue in the United States is inflation. If the US inflation declines quickly, what countermeasures does the Federal Reserve have? The biggest estimate is to raise interest rates. Will it cut interest rates? This is the most concerning issue for overseas markets and market investment. Of course, there are also some geopolitical influences that the market could be better at raising interest rates, including situations similar to Russia and Ukraine.

In short, you all have spoken quite thoroughly about the domestic aspects, and I didn't spend much time talking about the domestic aspects. I mainly talked about the international aspects. So just now, Dr. Xunlei Li, Dr. Haibin Zhu, and Dr. Ting Lu, you all spoke very deeply. I think it is crucial to find ways to boost confidence domestically, so the points just mentioned by Dr. Ting Lu and Dr. Bin Zhang are very meaningful. In fact, we are facing significant challenges. In terms of external demand, we are in the economic recovery process, but the overseas market is experiencing a noticeable decline. Therefore, from an economic perspective, it is difficult for export growth to continue.

As for the domestic situation, as you just mentioned, since our monetary policy is relatively loose and has not flowed into the real economy to be transformed into investment and consumption, this is still the key. In this sense, how to turn this proactive monetary policy and fiscal policy into effective demand, including investment and consumption at both levels, is an important proposition. Of course, this proposition is directly related to how to boost confidence. If confidence is boosted, residents will be more willing to consume, and enterprises will be more willing to invest, which is directly related.

Xunlei Li: I highly agree that the discussion is in-depth with the previous speakers. From an international perspective, the biggest risk is that the Federal Reserve's interest rate hike may not be in place yet. However, some US banks may be unable to withstand it, which may lead to a financial crisis, which is a bit worrying.

The Federal Reserve has explicitly stated this time that the inflation target is 2%, but it is currently still 5%. The recession expected in the US economy has not occurred. Overall, it remains relatively resilient. The concern is how much negative impact the continued interest rate hikes will bring under these circumstances. Domestically speaking, I think the Chinese economy is in transition. Also the traditional model seems to have reached its limit. Speaking of exports, the excellent performance in March is just a flash in the pan. The rising labor costs and the relocation of industries will further contribute to the growth of our exports. As for real estate, the urbanization process has also significantly slowed down, and a new model has not yet emerged. At this time, how to deal with this is a very serious reality that we must face now, including our banks, which are unable to lend on the one hand, and have large deposits from high-net-worth individuals on the other. Private investment in the first quarter was almost zero growth, and encouraging private investment is useless. Even improving the business environment may not have immediate results because the investment impulse of private investment comes more from the expected return on investment. The effect will be limited if the expected return on investment is low, no matter how you regulate or promote the rule of law and business environment. As Haibin Zhu mentioned earlier, the local government's debt space is insufficient, which I also agree with. In fact, our local government's hidden debt, plus our explicit debt, is not small. Developed countries' corresponding debt growth rate has rarely occurred in their development history. They became rich before they became old, and their debt grew after they became old. We are getting old before we get rich, and we also have debt before we get rich. This is a significant difference between us and Western countries. However, on the other hand, if we do not further increase leverage, or even without increasing leverage, it will be difficult to maintain economic growth, such as around 5% growth, in the future. Because in the past, our debt growth rate is about three times the actual GDP growth rate. If we want to maintain economic growth now, debts must grow. This is not a question of whether we want to, but a model that we have to choose. Of course, what is worth reflecting on is the quality of our debt, that is, the quality of growth still needs to improve. The projects we invest in may be more casual, and we may not have used the money on the cutting edge. This is something we must optimize in our future investment and need to be regulated. It is not that the quality can be improved by talking about improving quality and efficiency in fiscal terms. We need corresponding measures. The more realistic problem we are facing now is the debt pressure of local politics. If there is no clear direction and clear measures in this regard, the financing cost of local governments will further increase in the future. I think this is still facing uncertainty in the future. This uncertainty leads to the difficulty of raising expectations, and the difficulty of raising expectations leads to insufficient investment. This is a negative feedback. I hope to enter a positive feedback system. I will just talk about these.

Bin Zhang: Thank you, Mr. Xunlei Li, Dr. Haibin.

Haibin Zhu: There are two major risks in the world, one is geopolitics, the situation in Ukraine, we are not experts, of course, and now the war in Ukraine is stuck. Will there be any accidents in the future? It has a huge impact on the world, especially Europe. The biggest economic risk comes from the Federal Reserve. The current market consensus is that US inflation will decline, and the Fed's interest rate hikes are basically nearing the end. However, the current unemployment rate is still very low, and inflation is higher than expected. Is there a possibility that if we talk about macro inflation, the Federal Reserve will be forced to raise interest rates even higher, which will deviate from the current market expectations and may lead to an increased risk of recession in the United States in the next step? This is the issue that the market is most concerned about. I would like to supplement that during the investor conference held in April at the Washington International Monetary Fund and World Bank Annual Meeting, there was a questionnaire survey asking investors about their top concerns regarding China. At that time, the top answer was geopolitical risks and China-US relations, followed by the future economic policy direction of China, which is related to the continuous opening up of China that Dr. Lu Ting just mentioned, the equal treatment of state-owned and private enterprises, and the confidence of private entrepreneurs. The third concern was macroeconomic recovery and the sustainability of the recovery, and the fourth was the restructuring and relocation of global supply chains.

Based on this logic, what should the Chinese government do? First, in the current global context, especially in terms of geopolitics, global supply chains, and significant changes in globalization, we should try our best to maintain a relatively stable external environment. This involves our foreign policy and other types of policies, and we should still strive to maintain a stable external environment. Second, the confidence of domestic private entrepreneurs is the top priority of current policies. Thank you.

Bin Zhang: Thank you, Dr. Haibin. Now, let's welcome Dr. Lu Ting.

Ting Lu: I would like to add a point from an international perspective. After the rapid interest rate hike, the issue that banks are currently face is the duration allocation problem, which has gradually affected some banks from last year to this year and may have a more significant impact in the future, especially in the commercial real estate sector. 70% of commercial real estate loans come from small and medium-sized banks, which have not only duration issues but also asset quality problems, as many commercial real estate values have declined during the pandemic, especially in large cities. In the coming months, we can pay moderate attention to this impact on the financial systems of the United States and Europe from an international perspective.

Domestically, the main risk in the coming months is likely to be in the real estate industry. From various indicators, the real estate industry has shrunk by nearly 50%, and the shrinkage of private real estate enterprises far exceeds 50%. Dr. Haibin just mentioned the difference between private and state-owned enterprises very clearly. This will lead to a problem that the risks faced by private real estate enterprises in our country have not been completely resolved, and we should remain vigilant in this regard.

On the other hand, the downturn in the real estate industry has led to a sharp decline in local government land sales revenue, especially in first-tier cities. The impact on local platform debt is a crucial risk we must focus on this year and in the coming years.

If there are any policy suggestions based on these risks, I hold that we should still emphasize the need to increase the intensity of targeted measures in the current loose policies of the real estate industry. According to population inflows and differences in local economic growth rates, some areas, especially from the perspective of land, should moderately adjust and relax indicators. On this basis, some areas can moderately encourage the development of real estate, while others should not. From the perspective of local government debt, on this basis, some areas should increase transfer payments and simultaneously carry out more robust hidden debt cleanup according to local conditions. Some areas can achieve sustainable development in the future due to local real estate and other economic developments, while others may not be sustainable if they increase their debt issuance at this time.

Bin Zhang: Thank you, Dr. Ting Lu. Our time is almost up. I will briefly summarize the opinions of everyone, which may not be accurate. Combining the discussion in this session, we can see that everyone's understanding of the risks of the future external environment is relatively consistent. Everyone is still worried that although inflation is currently declining, whether we can achieve our target inflation is not yet certain. How much policy adjustment and how long it will take is also unclear. During the adjustment of monetary policy and the tightening of financial conditions, how much impact will it have on the financial system, and whether we have seen the end of it, the answer is no. There are different opinions on whether the economy will enter a recession, but we cannot rule out the possibility of some developed economies entering an economic recession. This is for the external environment.

As for the internal environment, everyone's views are also relatively consistent. We are indeed facing a significant problem in the operation of the macro economy. Our real estate and local platforms used to be two important forces supporting the growth of total demand and credit. Not only did they bring economic growth through investment, but they were also the engines of credit and purchasing power for the whole society. Both of these engines seem to have problems now. The real estate market is far from what it used to be, and there is no end in sight for the adjustment of the real estate market in the foreseeable future. The risks are still significant. As for how to deal with and digest the debt of local government platforms and whether to increase it in the future, there needs to be a clear view.

In such a context, if we cannot create a credit engine, there is no guarantee for total demand, and it will be difficult to rely on the growth of departmental income and the recovery of investors' confidence. Therefore, the sustainability of the economy and the endogenous driving force for economic growth still face significant challenges.

As Dr. Lu Ting mentioned, I don't know if my summary is correct, but our current recovery differs significantly from past recoveries. The external environment is different, the geopolitical situation is different, and the endogenous growth recovery power is also different. This may make our situation more complicated and challenging in the future, and we need more discussions and consensus from think tanks and forums like the Tsinghua PBCSF Chief Economists Forum to come up with better ways to help us face these challenges.

Audience Question 1: Good afternoon, professors. I am a part-time student (Heng Li) from the PBCSF of Tsinghua University, and I work in the real estate industry. After listening to the professors' views on the current situation of the real estate industry, I am quite worried and nervous. We all know that the real estate industry has implemented a high turnover, high leverage, and high return rate operating model in the past. However, our industry has experienced significant fluctuations in the past three years. So, to achieve healthy and sustainable development for the overall real estate industry and the large Chinese real estate industry, what kind of good model can be adopted? Are there any good ideas or suggestions for directions? Thank you.

Audience Question 2: Thank you, chiefs. I am from the second phase of the Belt and Road Initiative class. I would like to ask about the issue of whether monetary policy is failing. The chiefs have mentioned some points. I feel that both the West and China are facing the same problem of capital idling and monetary policy failure. In the end, can overseas inflation be controlled? Does the Federal Reserve face wage inflation in the so-called crisis as a structural issue? Many young people may not want to return to work after the pandemic, and labor costs may continue to rise, including the ongoing impact of geopolitical supply-side shocks, de-globalization, and anti-globalization. So, is inflation or stagflation the new normal in the West? However, domestically, we are facing another problem of insufficient demand. I would like to ask if monetary policy can solve this problem.

Audience Question 3: Hello, teachers! I am a doctoral student from PBCSF. I would like to ask about the recent hot topic of artificial intelligence or ChatGPT. Since new technologies are currently in the exploratory stage, I would like to ask what kind of imagination artificial intelligence, digital economy, or financial technology might have for our future economic development after real estate no longer drives the economy. Are there any good ideas to replace traditional manufacturing or traditional real estate?

Bin Zhang: The first question, Haibin Zhu will answer.

Haibin Zhu: Around 2017, if we look back, it was when the "houses are for living in, not for speculation" policy was first proposed, and it was also when we estimated the turning point of the overall demand for the real estate market. Since then, the real estate market has entered a stage of decline in total volume and structural change, with replacement or improvement demand rising. This may be a key focus for the industry.

In the past few years, real estate policies have experienced ups and downs, which may not be a good approach in hindsight. We hope to return to the long-term institutional arrangements proposed in the "houses are for living in, not for speculation" policy in 2017 as the focus of real estate work. If you have forgotten, we had some specific suggestions for long-term mechanisms in real estate policy in 2017–2018. One of them was land supply system reform, decoupling land supply from household registration population and linking it to actual population inflows and outflows. The second was multi-channel supply (commercial housing, affordable housing, rental housing) to meet the needs of urbanization, new urbanization, and the new replacement housing demand for migrant workers settling in cities. The third was the institutional arrangement of the real estate tax, which will replace land finance in the future. It has been five or six years, and we are still lagging in these areas. I think it is not too late to make up for the loss. From this perspective, establishing long-term mechanisms is still a key focus of our policy recommendations for the real estate market.

From a market perspective, we need to recognize the trend of declining total volume and structural changes. Moreover, from a broader perspective, the Chinese real estate market may gradually transition from the Hong Kong model to the Singapore model. In the future, the developer industry will definitely further consolidate, and developers' business model also needs to be further differentiated to meet the structural changes in the market.

Bin Zhang: Thank you. The second question is whether monetary policy is failing, and I don't believe in the failure of monetary policy. From international experience, other countries first use monetary policy when encountering economic difficulties. When monetary policy is used in terms of quantity, it can be seen that employment growth has a distinct recovery. Why do I think it won't fail? Not only based on these experiences, but also when the monetary policy interest rate is very low, it is equivalent to a significant reduction in your debt borrowing cost, and the value of stocks, real estate, or other securities you hold increases, which indirectly causes a significant change in your balance sheet. If you are willing to save, you may suffer losses and be forced to encourage some consumption.

The adjustments it brings, whether in the United States or China, are adjustments at the trillion-dollar level, impacting investment and consumption undoubtedly. I don't think it will fail. Of course, what I said may not be correct, and other chief executives can also exchange views if they have different opinions.

Haizhou Huang: I would like to supplement this on the second and third questions. For the second question, I also agree with Zhang Bin's opinion. It is too early to judge the failure of monetary policy. Taking the United States as an example, Greenspan said that there is a lag in the effectiveness of monetary policy, which is 6–18 months. So the Fed has been lowering interest rates for a year and is still being implemented. Moreover, the US CPI inflation has already come down, which is the first point. The second point is that to make monetary policy work, especially in response to inflation, there are three possible scenarios. The first is a better one, where the economy slows down, and CPI comes down, but it may be a soft landing or a slight recession, which is better. The second is that monetary policy may be too aggressive, or the economic response is faster, leading to a more significant recession. The third is while raising interest rates, changes in the balance sheet and other prices, as emphasized earlier, may trigger a banking or even a financial system crisis. The financial system crisis deepens the economic recession, and the economic recession further deepens the financial crisis, leading to a deep recession and financial crisis. In this sense, there are three possibilities from the perspective of fighting inflation. In plain terms, there is no such thing as raising interest rates without adverse effects. So the problem with American banks is just part of it, and people are worried that bigger problems may occur. In fact, inflation will come down, and GDP growth will come down. As for the current situation being affected by the COVID-19 pandemic, many people prefer to work from home. If you don't let me work from home, I will ask for a raise, which is understandable, and this is happening in some American companies.

If the United States enters an economic recession, it will be difficult to find a job. It is unreasonable to insist that the wage will rise if you don't work from home, although many people may take it for granted. In 1999, the NASDAQ in the United States was booming, and at that time, many IT industry employees in Silicon Valley demanded a more relaxed working environment. Of course, there was no concept of Work From Home, but at least they could not work on Fridays and dress casually. After the NASDAQ bubble burst in 2000, these people obediently returned to work and no longer made such demands. Having experienced this once, including what is happening in Silicon Valley now, some large companies have employees who work two days a week and go fishing, and the company can't manage them. I think all of this will change. Looking at the consequences of raising interest rates, if the consequences are severe, the market supply and demand sides will interact, and the labor supply and demand sides will have some interesting interactions. To put it simply about ChatGPT, technological progress brings about deflation, as the cost of doing the same thing becomes lower, leading to structural unemployment because some jobs will be eliminated. When Watt invented the steam engine, and electric motors came out, many industries that were done initially by humans experienced structural unemployment. This is inevitable, and overall it brings about deflation. However, deflation is due to increased efficiency, and the cost of doing the same job has decreased, which benefits the overall economy. Of course, it will bring about structural unemployment problems, which need to be addressed through social policies and other aspects. That's my comment.

Xunlei Li: I would like to make a few simple supplements. First, regarding real estate, people may underestimate the impact of real estate on the Chinese economy. After all, the real estate market has been bullish for more than 20 years, and once it declines, the duration may be quite long. We often ask what countermeasures we have, although in many cases, there are no countermeasures. We still need to pay more attention to the power of the market. China has done the best job in the world regarding real estate control so far without experiencing the steep declines seen in the United States, Japan, and, recently, South Korea. We should not expect better policies in this regard, but we should also assess the impact on the future economy and society.

Second, monetary policy is definitely effective, but we still need to pay attention to the liquidity trap, especially domestic monetary policy. The implementation of monetary policy is now quite obvious, but its effectiveness will definitely become weaker and weaker, and the marginal diminishing effect is also very obvious. The core issue is not how to implement monetary policy but to advance reforms. If we only focus on marginal changes, such as the current structural monetary policy, monetary policy itself is a macro policy. The effect of macro policy is to adjust the total amount rather than the structure. Adjusting the structure would mean planned economy, and are you smart enough for that? Can you know how to implement policies for current problems accurately? It is still challenging to achieve, so domestic currency idling is obvious now.

Third, in the era of ChatGPT artificial intelligence, we should not underestimate this era. This era is a technological revolution, and the impact of the technological revolution will be enormous. However, in the end, it will enable our economy to grow and labor productivity to increase. The technological revolution is not problem-oriented but changes the pattern of the world. In this regard, the uncertainty of the future is still relatively considerable. Thank you.

Ting Lu: I would like to add a little bit. I think I will talk about real estate. In the past few years, in terms of real estate policy, there have been commendable aspects, but there are also some lessons and many areas that can be improved. Including the high-speed transformation model in the past few years since 2015, which is actually related to the large amount of funds allocated to many lower-tier cities through planned economic methods during those years of monetization. In this way, although it did boost China's economy then, in retrospect, it caused harm to many places, including the entire Chinese real estate industry and many private housing enterprises. It's not that nothing can be done now. There are still many aspects that can be done.

In summary, render unto God what is God's, and unto Caesar what is Caesar's. On the one hand, we should focus on the construction of public rental housing, low-rent housing, and affordable housing. On the other hand, we should moderately solve some problems through market means, such as the necessity of implementing new housing price restrictions in many places, which has caused a considerable degree of distortion. Moreover, how to allocate land has become a key issue. As both Haibin Zhu and I mentioned earlier, land allocation is extremely crucial. Therefore, given the current situation of the real estate market, it is not entirely helpless, nor does it necessarily shrink by half within two years. If it does shrink by half within two years, this industry, which accounts for more than 20% of our GDP, still has many aspects that are worth rethinking and reconsidering.

Bin Zhang: Thank you, Dr. Ting Lu. Let's turn to the host, Professor Ju.

Jiandong Ju: Thank you, Bin Zhang, and special thanks to the five chief economists for their wonderful sharing. I also want to thank the guests who participated today. What is particularly important and meaningful today is the exchange of views, especially the exchange of different perspectives, which deepens our understanding of China, the world, the economy, and finance. I am also particularly grateful to the guests attending the conference and the online audience for spending this day with us and exchanging ideas.

Our "2023 Tsinghua PBCSF Chief Economists Forum" has come to an end. Thank you!

Index

J. Ju (ed.), *2023 Global Financial Turbulence and Economic Outlook*,
https://doi.org/10.1007/978-981-97-0206-0

GPSR Compliance

The European Union's (EU) General Product Safety Regulation (GPSR) is a set of rules that requires consumer products to be safe and our obligations to ensure this.

If you have any concerns about our products, you can contact us on ProductSafety@springernature.com

In case Publisher is established outside the EU, the EU authorized representative is:

Springer Nature Customer Service Center GmbH
Europaplatz 3
69115 Heidelberg, Germany

FSC
www.fsc.org
MIX
Papier | Fördert gute Waldnutzung
FSC® C083411

Kolibri 360 GmbH
Ferdinand-Jühlke-Straße 7
99095 Erfurt, Deutschland
produktsicherheit@kolibri360.de